GIVING UP
OR
PRESSING ONWARD

Written By Janet Blaylock

Edited By Brenda Willmore

Copyright Page

No part of this book can be used or copied without written permission to the author, Janet Blaylock.

Preface

I have experienced numerous trials throughout my life, but I continued to press onward so that I could meet my goal in life, which was to be a published author. Finally, in 2007, I reached my goal and, I will continue to press onward to have other books published and to help others with their writing.

In my book, I reveal the circumstances I have experienced in my life and how I kept pressing onward to find something that I could accomplish in my life. I also explain how readers can overcome their circumstances so they can reach their goals.

Dedication Page

I am dedicating this book to the following people:

My Family:

Gladys Blaylock, my mother, passed away on May 10, 1999. I have dedicated a chapter to my mother. Even though her funeral was a sad event for everyone who knew her, my father and his brother and family, who were separated for years, were reunited.

Arthur Blaylock, Jr., my father, passed away on June 15, 2005. I have dedicated a chapter to him. Even though his funeral was a sad event for his family and friends, I became closer to my uncle and cousins.

Larry, my brother, has been a help and encouragement to me throughout my life and during the time I was a caregiver for our mother and father. He's also married to Jan, and they have two children: Nikki, and Brandon.

My Mom's Family:

My mother's sisters: Aunt Alvena, Aunt Edna, Aunt Leola, and Aunt Carol have all been an encouragement to me through my mother's illness and death. Her only brother, Uncle Al, who preceded her in death, had been an encouragement to me.

My Dad's Family:

Uncle Orville, my father's brother, has encouraged me especially in my writing. He always asked me about my writing whenever we saw each other. As a result, I wanted to continue writing so I could have my writing published. I wanted him to see my published works. We became closer after my mother's death and my father's death.

His children: Bob, Barbara, Linda, Star, and Cindy, have also helped and encouraged me throughout my life and especially since our family got back together after my mother's death.

Barbara and I became closer in the last few years. I am thankful to her and her dedication to God. She led my father to Christ just three weeks before he passed away.

Cindy and two of her girls helped paint my kitchen and moved some furniture around to make my house different and more comfortable for me after my parents' death.

My Friends:

Brenda, who is a very close friend of mine, was a great help and encouragement throughout my book. She took time out of her busy schedule to edit my book so I could get it ready for publication. Brenda is married to Mark, and they have three children: Marcus, Mattie, and Matt.

I am also grateful to Sara, Janet G., Lisa, Cindy, and Linda and all my other friends who have encouraged me in my life.

Contents

Chapter One
A Roller Coaster Life

Opening her fourth letter, Megan cried out, "Not another bill! I can't handle this!" As she burst out crying, the phone rang. It was her best friend, Christy.

"Megan, what's wrong?"

"I've lost my job, and I have all these bills to pay. Everything is going wrong. I need some money."

"Bob and I have had some trouble, too. I know how you feel. We've been trusting God to help us."

"He can't help me. I don't think anybody can. All of my life, I've had failure after failure. I want to be free from all of my frustrations."

"You'll always have trials."

"I'm going to move to another state and leave all my struggles behind."

"Running away doesn't solve anything."

"I've got to get away from here," Megan insisted, as she shed tears.

In this passage, Megan kept getting bill after bill. She became upset because she didn't have enough money to meet her financial obligations. As a result, she wanted to escape. The only thing she thought of was to run away to another state. She thought things might be better somewhere else. However, she didn't realize that wherever she lived, she would always have trials. She couldn't escape her unwanted circumstances. Christy tried to help her, but Megan would not listen. She insisted on running away and leaving her trials behind.

Have you ever felt like Megan? Have you wanted to give up and leave everything behind? When the trials in your life become too difficult to handle, you probably wanted to escape like Megan. Nobody likes to have unpleasant circumstances in their lives. However, everybody has to go through trials no matter where they live. Instead of giving up, you have to learn how to cope with them. That is a difficult thing to do when you are in the midst of a trial.

Throughout my life I have experienced all kinds of trials and have wanted to give up several times, but somehow I managed to keep pressing onward. That is the purpose of my book. I want to reveal my life to you and how I coped with the trials I faced in my life.

My Early Years

In December 1948, my parents and I lived in the small house on a farm northwest of DeSoto, Kansas. I was a month old at the time. My grandparents lived in the farmhouse until they moved to Topeka in 1949. We moved into the farmhouse at that time. Our farm was located near the Kansas River.

On February 3, 1951, my parents had a son. They named him Larry. That summer, we were in the 1951 flood, which destroyed our crops. Water flooded our house inside and ruined my mother's piano as well as other things. We had to go in a rowboat from the house to the main road in order to leave because the water was so high. We moved into another place temporarily until they could clean up our farm so we could move back. Since I was two and a half, I don't remember that much about the flood. We were happy when we could finally move back to the farm.

Because we lived in the country, I took the bus to and from school. I started school when I was four years old. My kindergarten class was at the end of the hall, with chicken wire in front of the doorway. When I was older, my mother told me she was upset about the classroom situation and fought for a better kindergarten room. The following year, which was too late for me, the school had a new kindergarten room. I entered first grade that year.

Later on, my mother told me she should have held me back a year and repeat kindergarten so I could have had a better start. She also told me the kindergarten teacher didn't really want to teach kindergarten.

We enjoyed living on the farm. I had a dog named Lucky, and Larry had a dog named Teddy. Our neighbors gave us our dogs. We also had a puppy named Tippy. Teddy and Tippy were killed, but we still had Lucky.

A truck driver hit Teddy, and Tippy followed our mother out to the truck. Since Tippy was a small puppy, she didn't see him when she backed out the truck, she ran over him. We were devastated during those times because we loved both dogs.

We still had Lucky, and Larry and I enjoyed trying to teach him tricks. I remember trying to get Lucky to jump over a stick. We tried to nudge him from the back by pushing his rear over the stick. He didn't learn it, but we had fun doing it.

Larry and I also liked being with our father when he was working in the barn. We got to climb on top of the corn that was in the back of the truck. We liked helping our dad. Larry and I also had our own cows. Larry's cow was named Ann, and my cow was named Daisy May. I also had a white bull named Snowball. Besides these animals, we had cats, kittens, pigs, and chickens.

In May 1956, my parents decided to move to Topeka, Kansas. That was a difficult time for me because I had to leave Lucky with our neighbors. I wanted to keep Lucky, but my mother was afraid he would try to go back to the farm instead of staying with us. I didn't want Lucky killed, so I accepted the situation even though I wanted Lucky with me.

Moving To Topeka

We moved into our new home on May 20, 1956, which was the day of our parents' anniversary. In September, I was going to be in the third grade, and my brother was starting kindergarten. This was a different experience for me because our mother took us to school, or we walked since we lived near the school.

I still had trouble in school because of the difficult start in kindergarten. My mother decided to have me repeat fourth grade. I felt like a failure because of it, but my mother felt like it was going to be the best thing for me.

After elementary school, I went to Capper Junior High. That was a different experience, too because I had a locker and had to go from one classroom to another. I didn't stay in the same classroom.

Some of my classes were on the first floor, and some of them were on the second floor. One year, I sprained my ankle and had to wear a cast and use crutches. As a result, I left my classes a little earlier so that I could have time to get to the next class. That made it easier to go down the hall and up and down the staircase without the other students.

The summer before the eighth grade, I started teaching piano. My mother taught me how to play and how to teach. I enjoyed playing the piano and teaching it. It was a way that I could earn some money at home.

After I graduated from junior high, I went to Topeka West High School. I didn't like high school because some of my peers played tricks on me or teased me. One particular incident really hurt me. Someone called me up for a date. I was excited and got ready for the date. However, nobody came. That upset me, and I didn't want to date after that. My mother and I found out who played the trick on me, so we went to her house and confronted her. She apologized for her actions, but we never became friends.

I wanted to have friends and to date, but that incident caused me to have trouble trusting people. It seemed like people didn't want to be my friend. I decided I wanted to be alone and do what I wanted, which was go to school, and then come home and teach piano. I didn't have a desire to be around any peers.

College Life

However, things changed when I went to college in 1967, I started making friends with Christians. I first met Linda. She was in my physical education class. Then, I met other people, Steve, Gene, and Sara, who are still friends.

I belonged to a Christian group even though I wasn't a Christian at the time. Steve and I started dating. We were going to go to a Topeka West basketball game, but we ended up having our first date in the hospital. I became sick when I was getting my hair done and had to go to the doctor. The doctor had me transported to the hospital, which was across the street. Since a room wasn't available, I had a bed in the hall. They had a curtain around my bed so I could have some privacy. Steve came to the hospital for our first date. It was a date I would not forget.

Shortly after I met Steve, he introduced me to Gene. Steve and I were going to attend a Christian retreat, but he couldn't take me, so Gene and I went together.

Christian Retreat

On the way to the campsite, it rained so hard that we had to pull off to the side of the road underneath a bridge for protection. We also looked at the map so we could find out where we were going. That was a new experience for me because I didn't know how to look at a map and locate the directions of where to go. Gene finally had to take the map and study it. Once the rain calmed down, we were on our way again. We finally made it to the campsite.

When we arrived, we registered and had a meeting. Then, we took our belongings to the buildings where we were staying.

The next morning, we met in the main building and ate breakfast. After breakfast, we had a meeting. In the afternoon, we had free time to play games, fellowship, or do whatever we wanted.

Gene wanted to talk with me, so we met inside the building and sat on the sofa. He talked to me about God and asked me if I had accepted Christ. I told him I did when my parents, brother, and I joined our church.

However, at the time, I didn't know what he meant. I assumed I was a Christian since I went to church. Gene was satisfied with the answer.

After the retreat, Gene and I went back home. The following Sunday, he started taking me to his church. Then, he became engaged to Linda. I went with them a few times until I decided to go by myself. Eventually, I stopped attending the church and went to another one.

Learning About God

One night after an evangelist spoke, we went into a room, and he shared the Gospel with me. All I heard was God's Wrath. He showed me that if I didn't accept Christ, I would go to hell. I didn't want to go to hell, so I prayed. I also prayed because I was afraid of God. I didn't know about God's love or the true meaning of the Gospel.

I continued to date Steve. One day, we went to the library at Washburn so we could talk. He shared the Gospel with me from a tract he had. I wanted to go to the Union because I was more comfortable there than I was in the library. I liked being in places where there was some noise rather than places where you had to be quiet.

He told me we would go to the Union after I prayed, so I prayed. I enjoyed spending time with Steve. However, a year later, we broke up.

The Bible Study

In 1972, I met someone. He invited me to a Bible study. He wanted to meet me at the Bible Study. I wanted to go even though I wasn't a Christian because I wanted to meet people.

However, I didn't go at first because I didn't like going to a place where I hadn't been before, especially at night. When we saw each other again, he decided to pick me up for the Bible study. I would not forget that experience.

He picked me up, and we went to the Bible study which was in a large house. When I walked inside, I saw people sitting on a red-carpeted floor. I was dressed up and didn't expect to be sitting on the floor. However, I chose a spot in a corner, which was about the only spot available.

During the Bible study, we prayed, sang songs, and then Dick, the leader, taught us from the Bible. I sat there and looked around the room at all of the people who attended the Bible study. There were a lot of guys who attended the Bible study. I was going to enjoy this even though I wasn't that interested in learning about the Bible.

After the Bible study, I met another guy, and he invited me to his church the following day, which was Sunday. I was excited about that. (We dated for a year and broke up. Even though we had similar interests, he wasn't interested in pursuing our relationship in a romantic way. I became discouraged and didn't want to date.)

When it was time to leave the Bible study, I walked out to the van with the one who brought me. However, that was the beginning of a different kind of night. He couldn't get his van started. He kept trying and trying, but it wouldn't start, so we walked back inside and told Dick what happened. After everyone left, he took us home.

By the time I got home, it was later than I expected. My mother had been worried and wondered what happened. We hadn't known the guy who brought me for a long time, but he worked in a place where we knew the owners, so we trusted him. My mother was relieved when I got home.

I told her that we had run out of gas, and the leader of the Bible study, Dick, had to drive us all home. I knew how to drive, but my mother took me or Dick picked me up since I didn't have a car.

Later on, my parents helped me get my own car so I could be more independent. I wanted to drive to the Bible studies and church instead of depending on someone else to pick me up.

I continued going to the Bible studies at Dick and Laura's house. Dick also led Bible studies in Manhattan and Lawrence, so I went with them to both of those Bible studies. I enjoyed my time with Dick and Laura and meeting people in Manhattan and Lawrence. After I made friends in Manhattan and Lawrence, I began making plans before the Bibles studies started, so I wanted to drive by myself.

Searching For Success

I had a difficult time in college after a few years. I went part time because I couldn't handle a full schedule. I always had trouble in school, but I didn't know why until later on in life.

One semester I had to stay out a semester because of my grades. During that time, I didn't do much except teach piano, read, and watch television. I tried to go back to school the next semester, but I still had trouble. I finally gave up school and stayed home because I felt like a failure and didn't want to try anything else.

One year, when my mother was in the hospital, I stayed with her a lot so I could take care of her. I wanted to be with her and help her. Since I enjoyed taking care of her, she thought I might like to work in a hospital.

I went to the Personnel Office to apply for the nurses-aid training. They accepted me for the training, but it didn't last long. I did a great job on the written work, but they didn't give me the help I needed for doing the physical work.

As a result, they told me that I couldn't continue and needed to work with machines because I wasn't good around people. That upset me, but I tried a clerk typist training. After I graduated, my instructor told me she hoped I would never get a job. That really hurt me.

I couldn't believe how all of these people wanted to discourage me in everything I tried to do instead of trying to help me learn and encourage me. What was wrong? I thought people were to encourage others and not discourage them. I continued to be depressed. My life seemed like a roller coaster because I had some good things happen, but then something happened, and I became upset and depressed again. It seemed like nothing was ever going to work out for me. I wanted to succeed in something.

After that, I decided to go back to Washburn, but I still had trouble and gave up again. In the spring of 1978, my mother and I went to Lawrence, to Kansas University. She was the Guild Chairman of the Topeka and Lawrence Guild Auditions. I just happened to meet a piano teacher and wanted to take piano from him. I enrolled in the summer and enjoyed it so much that I wanted to go to Kansas University.

Finding Success

In the fall, I transferred from Washburn University to Kansas University. I moved into an apartment in Lawrence at that time so I wouldn't have to travel back and forth. When I started at Kansas University, I was a junior. I decided to work toward an Early Childhood Certificate so that I could teach in a preschool center or become a director of a preschool center. I enjoyed working with children and teaching them pre-academics, so I thought that would be a good degree for me.

I lived in my apartment for a year and then moved into a duplex because it had more space and a garage. I also had a washer and dryer hookup so I could do my laundry home now. However, I stayed there for a year and bought a house because I wanted to stay in Lawrence.

During my senior year at Kansas University, I became frustrated because one of my instructors wanted me to change classes with someone else (who wasn't a senior) so she could have the classes she wanted. As a result, I wasn't able to take the class I needed. My instructor also wouldn't help me with something that I couldn't do. She kept telling me I could, but she wouldn't show me how. I had trouble learning new things and needed someone to show me how to do it. I became discouraged and rushed out of the room crying. I couldn't understand why people wouldn't help me.

After that, my instructor I had for my Child Development course, which I made an A in, suggested I change my major and degree to a BGS Degree in Human Development and Family Life. Even though I couldn't be a director in a preschool center with that degree, I was glad that I changed it because I could graduate earlier than I would have.

In 1980, I bought a puppy to keep me company in my new house. He was a Boston Terrier. I named him Lucky Punchanello. His father's name was Punchanello, and his mother's name was Ruffles. I loved Lucky a lot. I also nicked named him Licky Lucky because he licked me a lot. I was also lucky to have him. A few months later, I bought another puppy I named Toby Kenobi, who was a Terrier/Chihuahua, so that Lucky would have a playmate when I was gone during the day. (You'll read more about Lucky and my other pets in a later chapter.)

Finally, in 1981, I graduated from Kansas University. I couldn't believe it. I finally succeeded in doing something. Up until that time, I failed at everything else I tried to do, so I was glad that I took my instructor's advice.

After I graduated, I started a day care in my home and continued teaching piano. However, in 1982, things started going downhill for me. I didn't have many children in my day care, and my piano lessons were dwindling. My phone bill was too high, too because I called my mother a lot. As a result, I decided to move back to Topeka.

Moving Back to Topeka

I found a house in a nice neighborhood that wasn't too far from my parents. In fact, it was in the school district where I grew up. I started a day care in August 1982. I took care of infants through school age. I enjoyed taking the school age children to the same school I attended as a child. I also taught piano as well as took care of children.

In 1990, I met a couple named Brenda and Mark, who had two children and one who was about to be born. They enrolled in my day care. We became close friends and remained close throughout the years. They are like family to me.

I also had Lucky and Toby with me. However, Lucky died in 1987. Lucky had seizures, and when I fed him, he had a seizure and choked to death. That really devastated me because I felt like I caused his death. I still had Toby, who was a lovable companion, but I wanted a playmate for Toby.

The next day, I found an ad in the newspaper about another puppy. I called the number, and they gave me the puppy. Her name was Abby. She was part spaniel/terrier mix, and I loved her lot.

She was so friendly, and Toby and Abby got along. You'll read more about my pets in chapter three.

Searching for God

In 1982, I started going to Dick and Laura's church they started a few years before. I enjoyed being back with them again. However, after a few years, Dick and Laura moved to Colorado. I cried a lot during that time because I was close to them and didn't want to be separated from them.

Later on, I heard about another church that met in the same building where Dick's church had been, so I started going there. I met Steve, who was an evangelist.

In September 1987, we got together after church. He asked me if I had ever repented of my sins. I didn't know what he meant at that time, so he explained it to me by walking one direction, turning around and heading the opposite direction. He showed me that we are walking away from God when we sin, and when we repent, we stop and turn around and walk towards God. I understood what he meant. He also asked me if I would want God if I didn't have any friends. I told him no. He knew where I was with God. I finally told him I felt like I had to do good things in order for God to love me. He told me I was getting honest with myself, and that I was trying to earn salvation.

Steve suggested that I not return to church or have any contact with people, so I could get alone with God. I felt hurt and confused. I thought I was a Christian, but I didn't know what to think.

I went home and called Dick. After I told him what happened, he told me that he had doubted my salvation for a long time, too. He told me he would be praying for me.

After we stopped talking, I wasn't sure what I was going to do. I couldn't contact anyone. I was alone. I felt like nobody cared for me. However, things changed after that. You will read what happened in a later chapter.

My Roller Coaster Life

After I moved into my house in 1982, things were going all right for several years. I did some remodeling, too, such as ceramic tile in the dining room. I enjoyed having my day care and teaching piano. However, in 1990, things started going bad for me. My day care started dwindling as well as my piano students. As a result, I didn't have the money to keep up with my house payments. I tried everything I could to get more day care children, but things were coming against me.

Two women who lived in the neighborhood came to my house to see how I set up my day care. They wanted to start a day care in their homes. My day care was in the garage. I fixed it up like a preschool classroom. They liked my day care area. One couple fixed up their garage like mine, only they had more income and could fix it up better than I could. The other woman turned her whole house into a day care. As a result, they got most of the children in the neighborhood, and my day care failed.

In 1992, the people I bought my house from evicted me because of my low income and not having the money to pay the house payments. I lost everything I had put into my house and my day care. I became more depressed because I had to move back to my parents' house.

However, later on in my life I found out the purpose for me moving back home with my parents. You will read about this in another chapter.

My life was like a roller coaster. I struggled for so many years to be successful, but I failed at everything I tried to do. When I graduated from Kansas University, I thought my life was going to improve. However, when I lost my house and job, things went downhill again. I was up one minute and down the next. I hated my roller coaster life. Would things ever change for me?

Chapter Two
Moving Back Home

After I lost my house in 1992, I had to move back home. That was the last thing I wanted to do. My brother was married and had his own house and two children, Nikki and Brandon, and I was still single and struggling throughout my life. I had been away from home since 1978 and wanted to be on my own. Since I had to move back home, I felt like a failure. I felt like I couldn't do anything and would never succeed at anything. I wanted to do something with my life, but I felt like I couldn't. I became depressed and didn't care what happened to me because everything seemed to be coming against me. I didn't have a desire to do anything. I felt like if I tried to do something else, I would fail again. I was also tired of living a roller coaster life. Why couldn't things go right for me? Life didn't seem fair. I remained depressed for a long time. I believed that nothing was going to work out for me because I was a failure. At that time, I didn't know why things happened the way they did. My mother helped me with the transition from losing my house to returning home.

We have a main floor, an attic that was finished, and a full basement that was not finished. My mother turned the basement into an apartment for me. She had her office area in one section of my living room area so we could spend time together. My mother taught piano and liked to write. She wrote her autobiography, which I am hoping to have published someday.

In the basement, I had a living room area, kitchen, bedroom, and utility room that had a bathroom, kitchen sink, washing machine, and dryer. My mother also spent time downstairs when she did her laundry.

In my kitchen area, I had a stove, apartment size refrigerator, shelves, microwave, and my kitchen supplies. My bedroom was located behind the kitchen area. A long curtain separated the two areas.

In the living room area, I had a sofa, some chairs, and a long desk where I had my computer and television. I also had my own telephone line. It was like my own apartment, which helped, but I still felt like a failure. Even though my parents and my two dogs, Toby and Abby, were in the house with me, I felt alone and hopeless. I couldn't understand why I was a failure.

I felt like God failed me when I lost my house and my job because I lost everything. As a result, I continued to remain depressed and developed a low self-image. There were times when I wanted to escape from these circumstances or to have something good happen to me.

Flashback

When we first moved into the house in 1956, my parents finished the attic, but they didn't have enough money to finish the basement. However, they did finish it partially. My mother had shelves built along the walls so that my brother and I could play on them.

My brother and I had our bedrooms on the first floor, but when we got older, we moved upstairs. As we grew up, we decided to move our bedrooms down to the basement. By the time my brother was in college, he moved out and lived in a dorm. I had the basement to myself except when he came home for the weekend. Later on, after my brother got married, he moved most of his things out of the house.

Back to the Present

I organized our shelves for my computer supplies. I decided to work as a full-time freelance writer and piano teacher. I edited and typed resumes and letters for people. I also typed the newsletter and other material my pastor needed for church. However, I was not earning enough income of my own as a freelance writer and piano teacher. I needed to find something else to do, but I didn't know what it would be.

My New Job

In 1994, I had a summer job, but it was going to end after a few weeks because it was only temporary. Right after that job ended, I started a full-time job for some friends of mine, Brian and Lisa, as a nanny. A few weeks later, that became a part-time job in the afternoon, and I got a part-time morning job in Lawrence as a nanny for another couple, Mary and Marty, whom I have known for several years. I also babysat for Mary on Saturday mornings, and later on I babysat in the mornings Monday through Friday in exchange for computer training.

Since Mary taught me how to use the computer, I wanted to do Desk-Top Publishing like she did, but I needed a computer. Mary and Marty bought me my first computer. Later on, I sold it and exchanged piano lessons for another computer that was similar to Mary's computer. Mary also gave me different software, books, and other supplies that would help me get started in my Desk-Top Publishing.

I have always wanted to help others with their writing, and to write my own stories and books and have them published. I am thankful that Mary and Marty could help me during this time.

I also continued teaching piano during this time. I had my own piano in the basement, and my mother taught her students upstairs.

When my mother didn't have a piano student, she would get supper. If I didn't have a piano student, I would get supper. Because of our schedules, we fixed casseroles a lot. That was easy to do, and we could keep the casserole warm until we were ready to eat supper.

My father watched television or went back to his bedroom to lie down before supper. He had worked all day and wanted to rest in the evening while my mother and I taught piano.

I began to settle in to my new environment even though I had some difficult times. However, I wondered what was going to happen next in my life. I needed a job because my jobs as a nanny stopped. I also needed to find a doctor.

My Physical Condition and New Job

In 1996, I started going to a new doctor. I met his dietitian, and we talked. She knew the director of the substitute office for the Topeka Public Schools, so she had me contact her. I did and filled out the application. In November 1996, I was certified as an emergency substitute teacher. I could not believe that I was going to teach school. I was excited about it and nervous because I had not taught in that kind of setting. It was difficult at first, but I enjoyed it. I was around children and adults. That was going to help me with my income even though it was not a steady income each week. Since I was an emergency substitute teacher, I was notified after the regular substitute teachers were called to work.

During this time, I developed some physical problems that I had not had before. My doctor told me I was borderline diabetic. He took me off of sugar, which caused more problems. I became weak and almost passed out because the sugar level dropped too low. After that, he had me eat some sugar but not a lot. I started feeling better, and then he diagnosed my condition as hyperglycemia with hypoglycemic reactions. My sugar level would get high and then suddenly drop too low.

I also developed asthma, which I had not had before. I had allergies, especially to smoke and other odors, but I had not had asthma. I had to use an inhaler so that I could breathe better, but I had trouble using it. I just couldn't get the medicine into my lungs right, so someone suggested I use a space chamber. I did, and that really helped me get the medicine into my lungs.

One time when I was subbing, my throat became really sore and swollen. I couldn't eat or swallow without pain, so I went to the school nurse, and we called my own nurse. I had to use my inhaler every four hours. That night, I continued to use my inhaler because I felt really miserable and hungry, but I couldn't eat. Finally, the next morning, I was all right. I was able to sub again.

My doctor did an allergy test, and I found out I was highly allergic to eggs, peanuts, oregano, soy protein, goats milk, and mung beans, I had always eaten eggs, peanut butter, pizza, soy beans, and other things with most of these ingredients. Now, I had to give up these things. I couldn't understand why I suddenly became allergic to these things. I had to find food that I could eat, which was going to be difficult. I also had a variety of food that I had a medium allergic reaction to and little to no reaction.

Again, I had to adjust to eating differently and making sure I didn't eat something I was allergic to. It was difficult for me to give up food that I had eaten all of my life. I just didn't understand what was going on with me and why.

However, I was glad that I moved back home so that I could take care of my parents, and they could help me when I needed help. I still wanted to find a church that I liked, but I didn't know where it would be. I also wanted to search for God and find the missing link to my life.

Even though I didn't know what the missing link was in my life, I was happy that I had my pets.

Chapter Three
My Pets

Lucky Punchanello

In 1980, I wanted to have a dog for a companion because I was single. I bought Lucky, my Boston Terrier, from a couple in Topeka who raised Boston Terriers. Lucky was five and a half months old.

The first night, I put a small bed with a mattress, a pillow, and a blanket beside my bed. I put Lucky in the bed and covered him up. I talked to him and tried to show him that he was to sleep in his bed, and I was to sleep in my bed. I rolled over and tried to sleep. Suddenly, I heard something, and I rolled over and saw Lucky walking along the side of the bed and pawing it. I picked him up and put him on my bed. He walked all over the bed and then licked my face. I put him back in his bed, talked to him, and then rolled over and tried to sleep. Shortly, the same thing happened. As the night passed, I kept trying to get him to sleep in his bed, but I gave up and put him in my bed so I could sleep. I finally got one hour's sleep that night.

Since Lucky's previous owners started to paper-train him, I continued to train him. I would put the newspapers in front of the back door and if he went on the papers, he received a treat. If he went on the carpet, I spanked him and put him on the papers. He learned quickly to go on the papers. Whenever I went somewhere, I put newspapers down, and when I stayed home, I took him outside. Every time he wanted to go outside, he let me know by scratching on the back door or by pawing me. When I asked him if he wanted to go outside, he turned and dashed for the back door.

Besides training Lucky to go outside, I taught him to obey my commands by using Behavior Modification. I would say "Sit," and if they didn't, I would take my hand and push his rear down and say "Good Boy." He learned quickly to sit.

I also taught Lucky to respond to words such as: ball, pillow, bye bye, Grandpa, protein, Mommy, blanket, and love Mommy. He knew me as "Mommy." If I said, "Love Mommy," Lucky came to me and licked me. He also came to me and licked me when I was lying on the floor pretending to be hurt. He probably thought that I was hurt or not feeling good. I wanted to teach him to help me in case I was hurt.

After that, I taught Lucky to shake hands using the same procedure. I also taught him to roll over and lie down. Every time he obeyed, he received a treat, and when he disobeyed, he didn't receive a treat.

Lucky also knew the following spelling words: cheese, eat, and treat. If I spelled these words, he became excited and went to the kitchen so I could get him some food.

As I mentioned in Chapter One, Lucky died in 1987, which was hard on me. He had epilepsy and had a seizure shortly after I gave him his supper. I still had a child in my day care, and I had Lucky in my bedroom with a gate across the door. Lucky was pawing the gate, so I knew he was getting hungry. I decided to go ahead and feed him. However, Lucky choked to death and died instantly. I didn't know he was going to have a seizure while he was eating. I became devastated by his death, and I blamed me since he died after I fed him. I called my vet and tried to talk to the receptionist, but she could hardly understand me. She had me bring Lucky over to them, but he had already died. I took Lucky home, and my father buried him in my back yard. Lucky was only eight years old when he died. However, I still had Toby, who was a joy in my life, too.

Toby Kenobi

Three months after I bought Lucky, I bought Toby, my Terrier-Chihuahua, from the Humane Society in Lawrence so that Lucky could have a playmate. Toby was three-months-old when I bought him. Since Lucky was paper-trained, Toby was easy to train to go on the papers and to go outside. When I left the house, I put gates to block the two doorways to my kitchen and newspapers on the floor. I wanted to keep them in the kitchen while I was gone. After I returned, I had double trouble. Not only did Lucky tear up the papers, but Toby learned to tear them up, too.

When I was home, I took them outside. Lucky already knew to go outside, so it was easy to train Toby to go outside. However, when I took Toby outside, he tried to play with Lucky, but as time passed, he knew what "going outside" meant. Later on, when Toby wanted to go outside, he stared at me or barked once or twice. I asked him, "What's Toby want?" After that, he ran to the back door.

Just like Lucky, Toby learned words. He knew bye bye, cheese, go outside, eat, treat, play, get up, where's Mommy, protein, Grandpa, Doc Steve, and Grandma. When I spelled these words: treat, cheese, eat, Grandma, and Grandpa, Toby came to me.

Toby also whined when he wanted something. When I was in bed, he tried to get my attention to take him outside. If I didn't respond, he would lie down and kick my side until I got up. Toby would also say "Uh Huh" when I asked him a question such as "Do you like Doc Steve?" Steve was their veterinarian.

One time Steve heard me ask Toby, "Do you like Doc Steve?" He heard Toby say "Uh Huh." Steve said, "I heard that." He was happy when he heard Toby talk. I also had a witness to my dogs talking.

I also had a special name for Toby. I called him Toby Hop Toad. When he was little, he hopped across the yard like a hop toad. He was fun loving character.

In 1993, Toby became sick, and my vet kept him in the office for a few days. This devastated my parents and me. Toby was 12 years old and a part of our family. Steve recommended I get a puppy to help us through this difficult time in our lives. I thought that would help even though we wanted Toby with us. We didn't know if he would survive or not. I decided to look for a puppy and found one at the animal shelter in Topeka. However, I couldn't bring her home until Saturday, two days away.

Finally, on Friday, Toby got better, and I could bring him home. I still had Abby and Toby, and on Saturday, I was going to pick up a third puppy. You'll learn about her later.

In 1997, Toby was in bad shape. He was not going to get better. That night, Toby walked over to my dad, then to my mom, and then to me. It was as if he was telling us "Good Bye." He knew he was going to die because he was in a lot of pain. His kidneys were failing. I called my vet, but he was gone, so I had to go to an emergency vet. My dad and I took Toby to the vet, and he told us that Toby was not going to get any better. He recommended I put him to sleep. I didn't want him to suffer, but I didn't want to put him to sleep either. Because I saw how bad Toby was, I told him to go ahead and put him to sleep. That was difficult for my dad and me. We took Toby home, and my father buried him in the back yard. We all missed Toby a lot.

Toby and Lucky's Fun Time

I trained Toby and Lucky using Behavior Modification. If they did something I wanted, they received a reward. If they disobeyed me, they didn't receive a reward.

Sometimes, when I said someone's name, they went to that person and licked them. I continued to increase their vocabulary, such as the word "stay."

I also saw them work as a team against "Mommy." If I was eating something, Lucky would get on one side of me and Toby on the other side. I wanted my own food, so I gave them a rawhide stick or some of their own food when I ate.

Besides learning my commands, I've seen certain characteristics in them. If I was holding Toby and someone held out their hands to get Toby, he would come to them just like a baby. Lucky also learned that trick.

They would also come to me if I was crying. This showed me they were affectionate. They seemed to know that I was hurting and wanted to help me.

Most of the time, they got along. However, I had seen jealousy in Lucky because I had him three months before I bought Toby. When I first brought Toby home, Lucky always wanted to be near me and didn't want Toby around, so I had to show Lucky that Toby needed my attention, too, and that he could be a friend to Toby.

When Toby came up on my lap, Lucky lay down on the floor in front of my chair and looked up at me. When Toby wanted down, Lucky got up and tried to get Toby. As soon as Toby went off by himself, Lucky got up on my lap.

There were times when Lucky didn't want Toby around me, but he learned to wait until Toby got down so he could get up. Sometimes, both of them sat on my lap. Every time Toby came up to me, Lucky came, too. I also saw jealousy in Toby because he would come to me if Lucky got my attention. Even though they were jealous of each other, I felt love by them. It was exciting to watch their personalities develop. They were like my "children."

Christmas Time

In December 1981, I came home for Christmas. Because Lucky was a part of our family now, he had to have Christmas presents like my brother, parents, and I. I just couldn't leave him out. Lucky got to open his presents first. I had wrapped up some rawhides and treats separately, so he could have several to open. He took the package and held it in his front paws. He bit into the package and worked with his paws and teeth until he had it opened. His "mommy" helped him some, but he did most of the work. Christmas was an enjoyable time watching Lucky open up his presents.

During our next Christmas, we had double pleasure. Toby learned how to open his packages, too. Watching Lucky and Toby open their packages and chew on their treats made our Christmas an enjoyable one. We never knew what those little characters would do next. Life with Lucky and Toby was never dull because they were always full of surprises.

Abby Ruffles

After Lucky died and while I still had Toby, I saw an ad in the newspaper about a puppy that sounded like one I would like. I missed Lucky, and even though I still had Toby, I needed a puppy to help cheer me up. I also wanted a companion for Toby. I called the people, and they gave me their address.

When I arrived and told them I was there to see the puppy, they opened the door, and Abby ran up to me. I picked her up and cuddled her. I wanted her, so I brought her home. She was a cute Spaniel/Terrier/Chihuahua mix, and I named her Abby Ruffles because Ruffles was Lucky's mother's name.

I had a lot of fun with Abby, and I trained her just like I did Toby and Lucky. She learned a lot of commands, too. She even learned "Uh huh" just like Toby did. She also knew the words and spelling words. She was my little princess. Abby was a fun loving little girl. Toby and Abby got along.

In 2003, Steve told me that Abby had a large tumor in her stomach. He said it was cancer. I cried a lot because I didn't want to lose my Abby. She was 15 years old and still full of love and joy.

Throughout the next year, it seemed like at times that Abby's tumor was getting smaller, but then it didn't. I kept hoping that Abby would improve. The one thing that Steve and I wanted was for Abby to die naturally so we wouldn't have to put her to sleep. That happened.

Abby died naturally on October 11, 2004. I just happened to move my mattress and blankets on the floor so that I could be with Abby. I laid her on a blanket beside me. Abby barked off and on throughout the night. Her barking kept my dad and me awake most of the night, but I knew she was in pain. I had a difficult time sleeping that night. In the morning, I heard Abby bark lightly and cry out. She died after that. It was so hard for me to lose her because she was a very loving little girl.

During the last few months of her life, my other puppy, Sadey, that I got when Toby died, took care of her like a "mommy." She would watch after Abby and let me know if Abby was caught somewhere and couldn't get out. I could see that Abby was getting worse. She didn't know how to get out of a corner or out from behind furniture and would whine. That's when Sadey heard her and searched for her. Sadey helped me find Abby. You'll learn more about Sadey later on in this chapter.

Penny Sue

Liked I mentioned earlier, in 1993, when Toby became seriously ill and was hospitalized, we were all devastated. We didn't want to lose him. Steve, my veterinarian, recommended that I get a puppy to help comfort us during this difficult time.

I went to the shelter and found a cute scrawny looking puppy. When I first saw her, she pawed the cage. After one of the workers let her out, I picked her up, and she licked me. I fell in love with her right away because she was full of love. She was eight pounds and eight weeks old. I saw other puppies I liked, but I liked this little girl.

However, I called Steve and asked his opinion. He suggested I get her because she was so lovable, so I decided to adopt her.

Since she had just arrived at the shelter, she needed to stay there for a couple of days for the owners to claim her. If they didn't come, I could take her home on Saturday morning, so I agreed to that. I hoped that I could take her home because she was so cute.

On Friday, we got a surprise. Steve called me and told me I could bring Toby home. The next day, nobody came after my puppy, so I could adopt her. I couldn't believe that I now had three dogs: Toby, Abby, and Penny.

I'm glad I could adopt Penny because she was a lovable puppy and would make us happy. Penny was the baby in the family, but I was shocked when I found out Penny wasn't a baby. After a short time, Penny grew and grew. I found out she was a Poodle/Chow mix and was going to be around 50 pounds. Toby and Abby were small dogs. However, Penny brought joy into our lives. All three of my dogs got along, and Penny was like a mother to Toby and Abby because she was bigger even though she was younger.

Tippy Maxwell

In December of 1996, Toby was still alive, and I had Abby and Penny. Some friends of mine gave me another puppy, even though I had enough with three dogs. The owners refused to take no for an answer. He was a cute puppy. The owners named him Max, but I wanted to name him Tippy Maxwell because he had a white tip on his tail, white paws, and he liked to tip over his water bowls, food bowls, and trashcans. Tippy also ended in "y" like my other dogs: Toby, Abby, and Penny. I couldn't believe I had four dogs. My parents also helped take care of my dogs and the expenses.

When my mother first saw Tippy, she said he looked like a teddy bear. He was a cute and cuddly puppy.

However, that cute puppy, turned out to be bigger than Penny. He was Sheep Dog/Akita/Irish Wolf Hound mix. He grew up to be around 85 pounds. I couldn't believe my two big dogs.

I also trained Penny and Tippy just like I did the other ones. They knew spelling words and commands like sit, treat, eat, come, shake hands, and other words. They were smart dogs, too.

Tippy knew where the treats, food, bread, and cheese were. When I said one of the words, he went to where I had them and looked up. He waited there until I got him what he wanted. Also, when Tippy went to the kitchen and barked, I asked him what he wanted, and he looked up at the counter in the direction of the treats.

One day, I moved the treats or bread to see what he would do. He was so smart because he knew where I put them. He was fun to have around because I never knew what he would do next. He was full of love, too.

All four of them started sleeping with me in the basement until one night Tippy attacked Toby. Then, my veterinarian wanted me to keep Penny and Tippy away from Abby and Toby. After that, Penny and Tippy slept upstairs in my dad's room. Abby and Toby slept with me. While they were outside, we watched them carefully. We had our hands full, but my parents and I loved all four of my dogs.

Sadey Marie

In the summer of 2002, my girl friend, Cindy, brought me a cute Chihuahua that she had. She raised Chihuahuas to sell, but she gave me the puppy. I liked her a lot and had from the first time I saw her. They named her Speedy, but I changed her name to Sadey Marie. Her nickname was Speedy. Marie was my mother's middle name.

Sadey learned a few tricks, too such as shake hands. She was a loving puppy, and she liked to lick me. She was also a helper.

As I mentioned earlier, when Abby was sick, Sadey would be like a "mother" to Abby. She would keep an eye on her. If Abby got caught somewhere and couldn't get out, Sadey would stand where Abby was located and bark for me to come. She seemed to like helping me out with Abby. Sadey seemed to know that Abby was older and needed someone to care for her.

Another thing that Sadey did was find things. One day, my dad and I were in the living room. He had lost his sunglasses, and we tried to find them, but we couldn't. We heard something in the hallway. I got up to see what was going on. I couldn't believe what I saw. Sadey was playing with my dad's sunglasses. We were thankful to Sadey that she found his sunglasses, but my dad and I never knew where she found them. Sadey has been a joy in my life like all of my other dogs. They were like my "children."

Cassie LuLu

When Abby died on October 11, 2004, my dad and I were devastated. My father wanted another puppy, and it had to be black because Abby was black. I saw a cute black Cocker Spaniel puppy advertised on the Internet that I fell in love with. The puppy was located near where I lived. I filled out the application and received a phone call that night. I told the woman what happened to Abby, and how my dad and I wanted another puppy that was black. She gave me the name of the woman who had the puppy. I called her, and I got the puppy the following day. I named her Cassie LuLu. On the Internet, her name was Cassie, but the woman who had her said her name was LuLu. I liked both names so I named her Cassie LuLu. She was six months old, very cute, and shy, but she adjusted quickly.

My father perked up when he saw Cassie Lu, (which is what I now call her). He still missed Abby, but he enjoyed giving Cassie attention. Sometimes, if Cassie didn't listen to me, I would call her Cassandra. She obeyed instantly then. After a few months of having her, she began to obey my commands more.

When I first got Cassie, she wasn't used to a pet taxi, but I continued to work with her, and she became used to being in there. Now she enjoys being in there. Cassie and Sadey both have their own pet taxis. For several months, they spent time in there during the day except when I let them outside. At night, they slept in their taxis so Penny and Tippy didn't bother them. Now, they sleep under my daybed where I sleep and get along great with Penny and Tippy. They enjoy being out and love playing together. They are in their taxis when I have to leave the house, but the rest of the time they are out. Sadey does eat in her taxi, and Cassie eats under my daybed.

Sadey also changed her role of being a mother to Abby, even though Sadey was younger, to being a big sister and playmate to Cassie. I enjoyed watching Sadey change her roles. She and Cassie got along. They enjoyed playing with each other.

I have enjoyed all of my pets that I have had since I first bought Lucky. I really miss the ones that have died, but I still enjoy the ones I have left: Penny, Tippy, Sadey, and Cassie. They are like my children since I was never married or had any children.

I accepted the move back home because I still had my own apartment and my pets. However, I had a difficult time adjusting, and I didn't understand why I had to move home with my parents until a few years later. I also didn't have many friends or a church I liked.

Chapter Four
Where Is God?

When I went to college and became involved with Christians, I started wondering who God was and what being a Christian was about. As I mentioned in Chapter One, I attended Bible studies at Washburn, and I went to a Christian retreat. I even claimed to be a Christian, but I didn't know what it meant.

Where is God?

I still felt like God was not in my life. I didn't know where God was or how I could reach Him because He seemed like He was far away. I also wanted to find a church where I could fellowship with other people and to be accepted. Because of different circumstances, I have gone from one church to another church. I wondered if there was a place for me.

I had been going to Dick and Laura's Bible study since March 7, 1972 and enjoyed being around people. The first night, I met Walt. We had a lot in common and enjoyed spending time together. He picked me up to go to church. I enjoyed his church, too.

However, after a year, we broke up. He wasn't interested in pursuing a romantic relationship with me. That was a difficult time for me. He's the second one who broke up with me. I quit going to his church.

At that time, Dick and Laura took me to their church. I enjoyed being there with them. I also became the nursery director of the church. I loved being around children and wanted to serve the church. However, I couldn't attend the church service because I was in the nursery every Sunday. That was all right with me because I loved spending time with the children.

Because of some problems in the church, Dick and Laura left and started their own church. I wanted to follow them, but they advised me to seek out other churches. At that time, I felt rejected and didn't know what I wanted to do.

I decided to go to another church. I went there for a year, and then in 1978, I moved to Lawrence and started going to a church there while I was living in Lawrence. I went to one church for a few times, and then I left there and went to another church.

When I moved back to Topeka in 1982, I started going to Dick and Laura's church. I liked being back with them. However, Dick and Laura moved to Colorado. That was a difficult time for me because I was close to them and didn't want to see them move away. I didn't know where to go after that. I was going to miss Dick and Laura.

In 1986, Jon and Debbie, who were close friends of mine, invited me to their church. The following Sunday, I went there and felt accepted right away. After a short time, I started typing the church bulletin, but that did not last very long. I felt discouraged after that, especially when someone else started doing the bulletin. I tried to accept the situation, but I felt like I failed.

Later on, I accepted things, and I soon found my purpose for being there.

A year later, on September 20, 1987, Steve, one of the pastors, talked to me about my relationship with God. I told him that I got angry a lot, and that I knew I had sinned. After that, he asked, "Would you still want God, if you didn't have friends?"

I looked at him for a minute and said, "Nobody has ever asked me that before." After thinking about his question, I said, "No. I wouldn't want God." Then, I told him I had a dream about people trying to earn their way to heaven.

He said, "Now, you are being honest about things."

I began to see what was wrong with my relationship with God, but at the same time, I was confused because I thought I had accepted Christ as my Savior.

Then, he asked, "Have you ever repented of your sins?"

"What's that?" I asked.

"It is making a complete turn away from sin and turning to God."

He explained what he meant by using body motions. He headed one direction and then made a complete turn with his body and went the other direction. Immediately, I understood about repentance and then said, "No. I haven't repented of my sins." I knew then that repentance was the missing link in my life. In the past, I heard about repentance, but I never understood the meaning.

He said, "You need to stay away from Christianity for awhile because you are using Christianity as a way to gain acceptance."

I accepted what he said, but I felt confused and decided to go home and talk to Dick, my former pastor, who had moved to Colorado.

When I contacted him and told him about my conversation with Steve, he asked, "Is there any hope without God?"

"No," I replied. However, I did not understand what he meant. I told him no because I figured that was the answer he wanted to hear.

After that, he said, "I'll pray for you, and I hope you will turn to God. You have struggled with salvation for a long time, so I hope you can get it settled once and for all."

When I hung up, I started thinking about the things Dick and Steve had shared with me. Unaware that I had not been following God, I was convinced that I had never accepted Christ because I believed I had to earn salvation, and I had never repented of my sins and turned to Christ. I felt like I would be going to heaven if I read my Bible, went to church, and did good things for people. However, good works is not the right pathway to heaven.

Wow! God Is Real!

On Monday, God showed me what hope was. He showed me that He is our hope, and that we look forward to seeing Him someday. As Steve requested, I did not go to Bible study or talk to anyone that week. On Saturday, September 26, I decided to go to the evangelistic meeting that my church was having at a park. When I arrived, I saw Steve and told him that I wanted to talk to him. He told me we would talk after the meeting. Before it started, some of us walked around the neighborhood and invited people to come to our service.

During our time together, I sat and listened to the songs and to Steve's message. I began to cry so much that I had to get up and walk away from the group for a few minutes. Elizabeth came up to me and asked, "What's wrong?"

"The songs are bothering me as well as what is being said," I replied.

"Janet, you are seeing how bad sin is," she said. After she shared a little more about God, she asked, "Would you like to pray?"

"Not yet," I said. "Steve and I were going to talk after the meeting. Right now, I want to sit and listen to him for awhile."

"Okay."

As Elizabeth and I sat and listened, I thought about my life and the things she told me. As soon as the meeting was over, Steve and I got together and talked. He shared the Gospel with me in a way that I had never heard of before. He told me that I needed to make a decision to repent of my sins, turn to God, and confess my sins and ask Him into my life.

On September 27, 1987, I made the decision to follow God. At the end of the service, I went forward during the alter call and told Steve that I wanted to accept Christ. He asked, "Would you still want God if you didn't have any friends?"

I said, "Yes because I know that God would not leave me like people do."

Steve had me pray and then he prayed. Suddenly, the burden I felt for years lifted from me. I knew I had accepted Christ as my Savior. This time I knew God was with me. Steve and I met occasionally so that he could help me to know God better and to grow in my Christian life. He also took me through a Discipleship course, which was a course that helped me to develop a personal relationship with God. We met once a week and became close friends.

One day, when I was studying for my Discipleship test, God showed me that when I did something wrong to someone, their feelings were hurt. He showed me that He was hurt when I sinned. I felt bad inside and burst out crying because I did not want to hurt God.

What Jesus did on the cross for me became more real to me, and I began to understand more of God's love.

My Purpose

Later on, I helped Ken, my pastor, organize the Sunday School for infants through five years. I enjoyed teaching the children because it helped me to read the Bible, and I came up with some creative ideas for craft projects. Because Sunday School was at the same time as the church service, I missed church during the two years I taught the children. As a result, I did not develop adult relationships, but I enjoyed the children and getting into God's Word.

After two years of teaching the children, Ken told me I needed to be in the church service, and that someone else was going to take over the Sunday School. That was hard for me because I didn't want to give up my children, but I had to. As I talked with Debbie, I realized I had placed them ahead of God. I felt secure and accepted by the children. I didn't want to give them up.

When I taught the children, I spent time with God so that I could be ready to teach them though the Holy Spirit. After I quit teaching, I started backsliding because I did not have anything to inspire me to spend time with God in His Word. I needed something to study and someone to help me be accountable to God.

Even though I accepted Christ, I tried to depend on people for love and acceptance. I still felt like I could not do things on my own.

Chapter Five

Being A Caregiver – Part One

Dealing With Death

In 1997, I had some major disappointments. My uncle, who was my mother's only brother, passed away. A month later Toby, my dog that I had for 16 years, was in bad shape. He was not going to get better. I did not want him to suffer like he was, but I knew it was going to be difficult. I finally had the doctor put him to sleep.

A year later, I had a severe upset in my life. My mother had a tumor embedded in her jawbone. We found out it was cancer. It devastated both of us.

I took her to the church I had attended so they would pray for her. It was the same day I found out she had cancer. We went inside, and one of the men prayed for my mother and for me. That was the last time I heard from them. Nobody came to help me out or called me to see if I needed anything or to see how my mother and I were doing. I decided that was not the church for me.

She had to have surgery to have it removed as well as part of her jawbone. She was 84 years old at the time of her surgery. She went through the surgery and radiation. The radiation ended in November around Thanksgiving. She had a difficult time with the radiation because she was worn out.

In December, she entered the hospital because she was sick. We found out she was dehydrated. She stayed there for a few days, and they released her. In January 1999, I took my mother to the hospital. They admitted her to the hospital again. At that time, the doctor told my mother and me that the tumor and cancer returned. The doctor told us that she had six months to year to live. That really devastated both of us because I did not want my mother to die. I wanted her with me forever.

We considered different options, but they said she wouldn't survive surgery again. We decided to bring her home so that I could take care of her full time. I was also going to Washburn at the time, and I was about to finish my BA Degree. My major was English with a writing emphasis. I was to graduate in May 1999.

Being A Caregiver For My Mother

For several days, my mother slept in a recliner that my mother's brother's wife bought for her to relax in. We also had hospice come and help me during this time. After a month, the hospice nurse suggested we get a hospital bed for her to sleep in. We were able to get one. As a result, I had my bed, which was an old-fashioned hospital bed, and her hospital bed, the recliner, and some chest of drawers in the room where she and I stayed during the day and night. I also began doing most of my studying upstairs so that I could be with my mother.

One girl came and helped with housework. She also stayed with my mother while I went to school. During the time she helped me, she had called the church to let them know I needed some financial assistance because I could not work. They did not help me at all. As a result, I quit going to that church. I could not be a part of a church who tried to get people to go to their church and then turn on the people when they really needed help. To me that should not happen in a church. People should help each other when they see a need.

In March, the English Department arranged for me to stay at home with my mother and to do my work at home. All I had to do was to take my assignments to school when I could. A classmate would take notes in class for me, so that I could study the notes. I could also do my tests at home.

During the time I was her caregiver, her sisters came up to visit and spend time with her. It was a difficult time for them, too. They could see how weak she was getting. I wanted my mother to get better and had a difficult time believing that she wouldn't.

The last two weeks of her life, she was in more pain and wanted to die. I had a difficult time with that because I did not want my mother die. Death became too real to me at that time. I was to lose my mother soon and did not want to. I wanted to have her around. I did not like to see her in pain, but I did not want to lose her either.

On Mother's Day, my brother came home to be with us because she wanted to see him. She knew she was going to die soon. She wanted to talk to him. She had both of us beside her bed and told my brother that she wanted us to remain close. She told him that I had not felt a part of the family, and she wanted him to be close to me throughout our lives. That was the last time she saw him.

On May 10, 1999, the day after Mother's Day, my mother passed away. As I leaned over her bed to hug her, I cried because I knew the end was near. She looked up when I raised up and closed her eyes. I was glad that I was with her during that time.

It was hard to let her go, but she was ready to go be with her Savior and Lord in heaven. I was so depressed that week. I was to graduate that Saturday, and my mother would not be there. She wanted to stay alive to see me graduate, but it did not happen. My father was still alive, but he did not want to go. I almost did not want to go either, but I did. I was glad that I went to my graduation even though it was difficult. A friend of mine also took video pictures so that I could have the video.

Fond Memories

My mother taught me how to play the piano and how to teach. I enjoyed learning the things that she taught me. I started teaching piano in 1962. She was always willing to help me and answer my questions.

She also liked to write. She wrote a music book for preschoolers and that encouraged me to write my own music book. I wrote a theory book for my students. I used both books to teach my students plus other music books.

My mother also wrote her autobiography, which I plan on having published someday. She was also interested in my writing and my computer work. She would sit in her chair and watch me type on the computer. She was amazed at what I was doing.

In November 1998, I started writing for Suite101.com. I developed a site on Detective Fiction Stories. I continued writing for Suite101 and developing other websites through them.

I started writing a book several years ago, when I lived in Lawrence. Over the years, the book has changed drastically as well as the title. The title of my book is *Strange Happenings*, which I will have published in 2007.

The main setting of the book is the farm where we lived before we moved to Topeka. I used the main buildings but added a lot of scenery, other buildings, and hidden caves under the small house that was behind the main house where we lived. I wanted to make it more mysterious and intriguing.

My mother edited the book and drew a plan of the farm so it would help me write the descriptions. I enjoyed working with my mother on my book.

Another fond memory of my mother was the times we spent playing games. We liked playing Scrabble, and she was good at that game. Sometimes she was too good. In other words, she beat me. I am glad that we had that time together. We also played other games, but she enjoyed Scrabble more.

Everyone who knew her will remember my mother. She was a good, kind person, and wanted to help encourage others.

Chapter Six
Being A Caregiver – Part Two

In April 2002, my father became seriously ill. I called an ambulance, and they took him to the hospital. I followed as soon as I could. I stayed there with him most of the night. They told me he was severely dehydrated, and they almost lost him in emergency before I got there, but he survived. I was glad about that. because I did not want to lose my dad. It was difficult enough losing my mother.

They transferred him to a private room and began immediate care. I stayed there most of the night. However, my father wanted me to go home and take care of the dogs. He loved my dogs, and they knew him as Grandpa and my mother as Grandma.

I spent time with my dad at the hospital and helped him during his stay. When they released him from the hospital, they transferred him to Rehab so he could learn to walk again. Within a few weeks, he was up walking and doing better. A month later, they discharged him. He came home so I could take care of him. I wanted to be with my father, and he wanted to come home and be with my dogs and me.

I loved my father and wanted to be his caregiver like I was for my mother. He continued to gain his strength and was doing better. I went back to being a substitute teacher in the fall.

In December 2002, my father had a major stroke. He was in the hospital for a few days and back in Rehab for a month. I stopped working as a substitute teacher for so I could be with my dad in the hospital. I wanted to spend time with him because I did not know how much longer I would have with him.

He survived the stroke again and could walk better, but he had to come home in a wheel chair. A physical therapist worked with my dad at the house a few days a week to help him walk. An occupational therapist came over to work with his hands. My dad was paralyzed for a short time on the right side. He overcame most of his disability. However, he could not use the right hand as he did before. He used the left hand to eat and do things.

Since my dad had his stroke, I did not want to continue subbing, but I did renew my certificate each year so that I could sub again in the future. My desire at the time was to stay home with my father and be his caregiver. I never knew when he was going to have another stroke, so I did not want to leave him for a very long time. My dad continued to improve, but I still stayed at home so I could help him.

My New Job

In 2002, I started a new job at home. I became an online tutor. I enjoyed tutoring online, but it was different than teaching in a classroom at school. They hired me in November, but that didn't last long because they had several students who were very rude and didn't want to learn. They also gave me subjects that I couldn't tutor in, so the student's didn't give me a high evaluation.

As a result, they let me go. I found out later that they fired other tutors, too. I didn't like the company because of the way they treated people.

I found another company that I really liked and started working for them in 2002. I enjoyed working at home so that I could be with my dad and help him when he needed help and to be with my dogs.

Things worked out for me for the next three years. I enjoyed tutoring online and working as a freelance writer. However, another major upset came about in 2005.

My Father's Accident

My father fell and was in a lot of pain. I called for an ambulance, and they got him and took him to emergency. I followed them and stayed with my dad the whole night. I find out that he broke his hip in three places and had to have surgery. He was 87 at the time of his surgery. He fell on May 22, 2005, and his surgery was May 23, 2005. That was a difficult time for me because I felt responsible for his fall. I kept thinking if only I had been there he would not have fallen. I cried a lot during this time because I did not want to lose my dad, too.

We had not had a close relationship until after my mother passed away in 1999. Then, my father and I started to develop a closer relationship even though we had several difficult moments.

A Happy Reunion

My dad and his brother, Orville, had not spoken for several years because of the bitterness that developed in their relationship. My aunt, uncle, cousins, and I were brought back together the day of my mother's funeral. That was a very difficult time because I lost my mother, but it was also a good time because my dad's family and I were reunited.

My dad still had bitterness towards his brother and did not want to see him, but things changed the day of my dad's surgery. My uncle and two of my cousins, Cindy and Barbara, came to be with me at the hospital during my dad's surgery.

Accepting Christ

When they took my dad to the pre-op room, I watched out for my cousins and uncle. They arrived just in time. My cousin, Barbara, stood right beside my dad's bed, and her father sat in a chair beside the bed. My cousin shared the Gospel with my father. He acknowledged at that time that he was a sinner. He prayed to accept Christ as His Savior and Lord. I could not believe what I witnessed. My dad was going to heaven after he passed away. He and my mother were going to be together again for eternity.

After they took my dad to surgery, my uncle, cousins, and I went down to the hospital cafeteria. They and bought my lunch and their lunch. We had a good time together even though it was a difficult time for us with my dad in surgery. We were thankful that he accepted Christ as his Savior and Lord.

When my dad's surgery was over, we talked to the doctor, and then my uncle and cousins had to leave. I went upstairs to my dad's room to spend the day with him. I did not want to leave him that day, but he wanted me to go home and take care of the dogs, so I did.

I got up early the next morning and packed up a few things that my dad needed and what I wanted to take to the hospital to work on during the time I was there. I continued going there for about a week, and them they transferred him to Rehab.

Later on, they transferred him to a nursing facility that had extended Rehab. He was there on a Saturday, and on Sunday, I noticed something was wrong, but it did not dawn on me what it was.

On Monday, someone from the nursing home called me. They told me my dad became worse so they called for an ambulance to come and take him to the hospital. I rushed over to the nursing home and followed the ambulance to the hospital.

After the doctor at the hospital checked him out, I found out that his organs were failing. This upset me a lot because I wanted my dad with me. I did not want to lose him, too. I did not want to be alone. They kept him in the hospital and treated him. However, on June 15, I knew in my heart that he was going to die. I arranged to stay at the hospital in his room because I did not want to leave him.

That day, was a difficult time. I met someone in the elevator and started telling him what was going on because he knew something was wrong with me. He had asked me if I was all right. He walked with me to the hospital cafeteria. He bought my lunch and carried it to my dad's room.

During the day, my dad hollered out for his brother. I immediately called my cousin, Barbara, and they came to the hospital to be with him. My other cousins also arrived at the hospital to be with my dad and me. They arrived around 8:00 and stayed for about 45 minutes. Then, another cousin-in-law came to be with me, too. He stayed while the other ones went to visit another relative of theirs (not my relative).

I planned on staying at the hospital that night because I believed my father was going to pass away that night. I was glad that my uncle and cousins came to the hospital to see my dad. That helped a lot.

About 11:45 PM, my father passed away. I was glad that I was with him. The nurse had just taken his vital signs and everything was fine, but the minute she left, he died.

I went to the nurse's station and told them about my dad. They were shocked because the vital signs were good. Four of the nurses entered the room. The charge nurse felt him and pronounced him dead. That was when everything became real to me. I knew he was gone but just hearing it from them made it so real.

They called my cousin and my brother. My cousin lived in town, and my brother live about two hours away from me. My cousin came to the hospital to help me gather up my things and to follow me home. I did not want to leave my dad, but I knew I had to. I had a difficult time going home and being by myself, except for my dogs. I cried a lot that night and could not sleep. I missed my dad. I also cried for the dogs because they would not see their grandpa again. They loved him, and he loved them.

My brother came up the next day to meet with Doug, the pastor who was going to do the service, my cousin, Barbara, the funeral director, and me. Before my dad passed away, I had asked Barbara to help me out since she lived in town. I was glad I did. Barbara organized the music for the funeral and the meal after the services. I appreciated everything she did for me. My brother took care of the business side of things like life insurance, and helped with the decisions about the casket, and cemetery arrangements.

Several of my cousins went to Topeka Bible Church, and I had just started going there so I asked Doug, one of the pastors, to do the service. He told me he felt honored that I wanted him to do my father's service. Two days before my dad passed away, Doug came to the hospital to meet my dad and visit with him.

In 2002 after my dad got out of the hospital, we went to see our lawyer. He wanted to change his will and add my name to the deed of the house. My brother was married and had his own place, so my dad wanted me to have my own place. When my dad passed away, the house would be mine.

When my dad had my name put on the house, it showed me that my dad cared for me even though we had several difficult moments throughout my life.

The day after my dad passed away, I had everything changed into my name. I also changed my phone number and had it unlisted because I did not want a lot of phone calls. I wanted to be alone with my dogs.

Fond Memories

During the time my dad and I were together, I had a desire to teach him to play games like Connect Four. He really liked that game.

In the evening, we would play that game and watch television. We ended up playing the game for four hours. I could not believe he wanted to play that long. I was getting a little tired, but he wanted to continue playing. We also ate snacks while we played. We enjoyed our time together.

We had not had that kind of relationship in the past, so it felt good to get to know my dad during this time. I was also glad that I taught him how to play the game because it gave us something to do together. Normally, he would have gone back to his bedroom instead of staying up and watching television or playing games.

Another time that I enjoyed was when he made it possible for me to get a new computer. When I brought it home, he sat in his chair and watched me take it out of the box. He wanted to help me if I needed him to. He enjoyed watching me put the computer together.

I had moved my office upstairs to a corner of the living room so that I could be closer to my father if he needed my assistance. I did that when he almost passed away in 2002. It helped having my office upstairs because he became interested in what I was doing. He also watched me tutor my students online while he watched television.

Another sad but happy moment was when my dog, Abby, died. She had cancer in 2004. My veterinarian did not expect her to live as long as she did. Abby died in October 2005. My dad and I went through a difficult time because Abby was a part of the family for 16 years. We missed her a lot. My dad had become depressed for about two weeks and did not want to eat much at all. I tried to encourage him to eat so he could keep up his strength. He finally told me he wanted another puppy, and it had to be black. I still had Tippy, Penny, and Sadey, my Chihuahua, but he wanted a black puppy. My girl friend, Cindy, gave me Sadey the summer of 2001. She was a little over a year when I got her.

I tried to locate a black puppy for about two weeks. Finally, I searched the Internet and found a black puppy named Cassie. I filled out the online application when I found out the puppy lived close to me. I received a phone call that night. The woman gave me the name and number of the one who had Cassie. I found out that her name was LuLu, and the name Cassie was not right on the Internet. I liked both names, so I named her Cassie LuLu. I got her the next day, which was Sunday.

Cassie was six months old. My dad liked her, but he still missed Abby. Cassie looked a lot like Abby. She was all black and had some white on her paws and stomach. Abby was black with some brown areas. They were both cocker spaniel mixes. It was like having Abby back with me. We enjoyed having Cassie as a part of the family.

Sadey also liked Cassie. They enjoyed playing together because they were closer in size than Tippy and Penny. Tippy and Penny spent time together.

My dogs have also missed their grandpa. When I first came home, Tippy and Penny could not understand why they could not go into the room where their grandpa used to be.

I had a gate across the doorway so they could not get in. I didn't want the big dogs in the same room with the smaller ones. Everything was all right for for awhile. I put down Penny and Tippy's water bowls and treats for them to have during the night. However, around 3:30 AM, they barked and couldn't settle down. They wanted their mommy with them.

I got up and slept on the daybed that I brought down from the attic and put in the living room for a sofa since my brother took the sofa and a few other things from the inheritance he received. I stretched out on the daybed and put Sadey and Cassie in their pet taxis. Penny and Tippy slept beside my bed, and they were happy since they got to be with me. They wanted to be with me at night because they missed their grandpa.

After that, I tried to sleep in my room, but they continued waking me up, so I decided to sleep on the daybed. It has worked out great ever since.

I will remember my dad forever. I know that I will see him in heaven someday. If he had passed away in 2002, he would not have gone to heaven. I am glad my cousin, Barbara, led my dad to Christ so he could be in heaven with my mother and the rest of our family who has accepted Christ for eternity.

Chapter Seven
Living Alone

Since June 16, 2005, I knew why I had to move back home in 1992. The house was to be mine. I was back to living alone, but it was the beginning of a difficult time for me because I did not know what to do without my parents. I still had my brother, but he was married and had a family. He also lived two hours away, so he did not come up very much to visit. I was alone. All I had was my dogs, my online tutoring, my substitute teaching, and my piano student. I had my own house, which was paid for, but I needed to have a steady income so that I could meet my bills.

My dad and I had been living on his social security. Now that he was gone, I did not have that income. I was on my own and didn't think I would survive without someone with me who could help me through my difficult times.

Remodeling Time

However, the week my dad passed away, things changed in my life. My cousin, Barbara, whom I became close to again, came over. We cleaned up my living room, kitchen, dining room, and bathroom. I could not believe what was happening. I enjoyed the company and the improvements we did in the house, but I still missed my dad.

Barbara and I first cleaned up the dining room. We removed the old carpet and cleaned up the floor and put down new area carpets in the dining room. Barbara and I also cleaned up the kitchen. We decided to paint the kitchen walls so that I could have a new place that was just my colors and what I wanted. She put on the prime first and then one coat of the cocoa mocha. We went from a lime green to a cocoa mocha. It made such a difference in my kitchen. It was brighter and cheerful looking.

The next day, Barbara's sister, Cindy, and her came over to paint. Two of Cindy's girls also came over to help. They had another surprise for me. They brought up the dresser and my kitchen table and chairs I had in the basement. We switched my bedroom into my dad's room, which was larger. We moved the kitchen table and chairs that my brother inherited onto the back porch that was enclosed.

My kitchen was becoming like new. We liked it a lot better because it made the kitchen brighter. Now that we had new walls, we needed to get new curtains. We could not find any that would fit the windows, so Barbara ended up making new curtains. We looked for material in one store, but we could not find any. We finally found what we wanted at Wal-Mart. We bought the material, and Barbara took it home so she could make the curtains. She also had enough material left to make a tablecloth. I really liked my new kitchen.

Now that I had a new kitchen, I needed a new dining room, living room, and bathroom. Barbara and I decided to paint the hallway, living room, and dining room, too. We also had help from my friend, Brenda, who is like a sister to me. All three of us painted the three areas. Brenda and I also bought white blinds and burgundy silk curtains for the windows to go above and down the sides of each set of windows in the dining room and living room. My favorite color was blue, but once I saw the curtains up in the rooms, I liked the color Brenda and I chose. It looked great with the light pink walls.

I still missed my parents. We had lived there since 1956, and before my dad passed away, he made it possible for me to keep the house so I could live there. We hadn't done much remodeling over the years, but things were changing now.

Someone gave me some money so I could do some more remodeling. I had new vinyl on the kitchen and bathroom floors, a new furnace, new water heater, new plumbing, new sewer system, a new vanity in the bathroom, and I replaced the bathtub with a walk-in shower. I was amazed at the things that were happening in my life.

Difficult Times

I continued my work as a freelance writer, online tutor, substitute teacher, and a piano teacher. I enjoyed everything I did, but at times I didn't have enough money to meet my financial obligations. That made it difficult for me to trust God. Even though I had trouble trusting God, He came through.

God also provided a closer relationship with my cousins and my girl friend, Brenda, who is like a sister to me. My cousin, Barbara, and I are closer than we had been before. They have been there to help me through my difficult times.

I thought I was going to be alone after my parents passed away, but God provided friendships with other people at church and a closer relationship with my cousins, and my friend, Brenda.

Holidays

The holidays were the most difficult time to overcome. My father passed away just before Father's Day. My mother had passed away the day after Mother's Day. Those two days are difficult for me. On Father's Day, my cousin, Barbara, invited me to spend the day with the family and celebrate it with my uncle and cousins. That helped a lot because I enjoyed getting acquainted with my second and third cousins, whom I haven't known for years. However, I still missed my dad because it was my first holiday to be without him.

Thanksgiving and Christmas were also going to be hard. I was going to be alone on those two days. I did not want to be alone, but that is what I thought was going to happen. However, things changed. Barbara invited me to spend time with the family for Thanksgiving and Christmas. This also helped me during this difficult time.

I was not sure how I was going to make it financially because of being alone. The house was mine, and my responsibility for paying the bills. I didn't know how I would be able to do that with the income I had been making. However, God had everything planned. He provided the money I needed. People gave me money after my father's death to help me meet some of my financial obligations. God also provided the money I needed to help me out since that time. He even provided a cheeseburger when I prayed for one.

God has provided for me throughout that time. I still went through difficult times when I felt like God wasn't going to provide for me, but He came through.

In 2004, I began attending another church that I really liked. I felt accepted there and some of my cousins were members there. I enjoyed being with my cousins and the services. I also went through a Welcome Class to find out more about the church. In 2005, I became a member of the church.

Chapter Eight

Trials! Let's Escape

Trials Are All Around Us

Trials are all around us--Conflicts with people, job, school, finances, or physical problems. When you have too many problems, like Megan did in the story I mentioned in Chapter One, you have a tendency to run away. You want to escape from your circumstances in your lives, but that is not the way to handle your trials. You probably wish you didn't have any unpleasant circumstances in your life, but life doesn't work that way. You need to learn how to cope with your trials.

Life would be different without trials. Imagine yourself in a world free from trials. Everything is perfect--no conflicts, no financial problems, no sorrow, no pain, no physical problems, or death. Would you like to be in a place like this? That is what heaven will be like, and what the world was like before Adam and Eve sinned. However, because of sin, we have trials and difficult times in our lives. We just have to learn how to cope with them.

A Deserted Island

Now, imagine yourself on a deserted island. That would seem like a good place to be because you probably think you would not have any trials. However, you are wrong. Let's think about the trials you might have on a deserted island.

What about eating or buying material possessions? Do you like to go to restaurants and eat? Do you like to go to grocery stores and buy the food you need to fix at home for your meals? If you can answer **YES**, then you would not be happy on a deserted island.

I know I wouldn't be happy living on a deserted island. However, there were times when I felt like I wanted to escape from my unpleasant circumstances because people criticized me throughout my life. On the other hand, I wouldn't have the material possessions I needed and were used to having.

If you were on a deserted island, you wouldn't be able to go to restaurants or to fix anything you wanted to eat. The kind of food you'd have available would be seafood, fruit from trees, or meat, if you had a way to kill the animals and cook them. You wouldn't be able to go shopping for food, clothes, or other material possessions. Would you be happy if you couldn't buy these things? You probably wouldn't be happy because you were used to the conveniences of stores and cooking your meals at home. If you were away for a day or two, then you might be happy, but not for a long time.

What about a place to stay? Do you think you'd have a place to live on a deserted island? You might if you brought a tent or their happened to be a cabin or a cave on the island. Would you feel safe in the bad weather if you just had a tent? What would you do if a strong wind blew your tent over? A storm could also tear holes in your tent and cause rain to come inside.

Since you'd be near the lake, you could be flooded out if a thunderstorm came. Does this sound like a place you would want to be? You would probably agree that it was not a good place because of the trials you would experience.

Another problem you would experience is loneliness. You would be alone on a deserted island. You would have to deal with that as well as other emotions. Are you used to having family or friends around? Do you think you could handle being alone on a deserted island by yourself with nobody to talk to? You would probably say **No**.

You need family and friends with you for support during your difficult times. However, you cannot depend on a specific person to help meet your needs.

Living in a Mansion

Now let's see what would happen if you lived in a mansion and had everything you could possibly want. Would you be happy in this lifestyle? Do you think you would have any problems? No matter what kind of lifestyle you have, you would always have problems.

You could have a proud spirit because you would think of yourself as someone important. However, you would still have to pay your servants, utilities, and other bills. Your servants would do things for you, and you could become lazy. If something happened to your business that was unexpected and you lost everything, then how would you feel?

Your answer to that question will show your proud spirit if you became depressed. You would also place too much value on material possessions. You would have to start over again by finding another job and another place to live. Even if you did not live in a mansion, you could still lose your job and your house.

Now we are going to look at various ways people have used to try and escape their trials. Have you used any of these ways to escape?

Temporary Ways to Escape Trials

People have used different ways to escape their trials. (1) Giving up--Depression, (2) Sleeping, (3) Television, (4) Eating, (5) Shopping, (6) Sinful Activities, (7) Prescription and Non-Prescription Drugs, (8) Alcoholic Beverages, (9) Running Away, and (10) Suicide. All but the last one are just temporary ways to escape.

(1) Giving Up – (Depression)

Imagine yourself sitting in your chair or lying in bed. You are focusing on your favorite television show. Your mind becomes distracted, and you find yourself dwelling on your unpleasant circumstances. You try watching your television show, but you become more distracted by your thoughts.

As you are sitting in your chair or lying in bed, all of your thoughts start to overwhelm you. You become restless and try focusing on your television show, but you cannot concentrate. You may even get up and wander around the house in search of something. Maybe you go to the refrigerator thinking food might help.

You search for something to eat and drink. Then, you go back to where you were and try focusing on the television show as you are relaxing and eating your snack. However, your thoughts start to overwhelm you again. As a result, you become worried, tense, nervous, stressed out, and depressed. Nothing seems to help.

Finally, other emotional problems arise--such as an unhealthy self-image, hopelessness, bitterness, jealousy, anger, pride, rejection, and discontentment. Eventually, you give up or find another way to escape. Would you like to live your life this way? The answer is **NO**.

My Experience

As I mentioned in a previous chapter, I was a day care provider. During that time, I became depressed when a parent stopped my day care services because of a minor incident. I felt like I failed again. If parents had been willing to discuss their concerns with me, things might have worked out.

I believed in discussing any concerns that I had or that parents may have had so that we could work out problems. However, people were not always willing to express their feelings. When they expressed their concerns, we worked out a solution.

When parents quit my day care, I became depressed again because I needed the income to meet my financial obligations. I had several bills to pay including house payments, insurance, and utilities. I started getting behind on most of my bills because of the lack of income.

I wanted to please people, but I felt like I had to be perfect in order for anyone to like me and to continue in my day care. Because of that feeling, I had a lot of stress in my life. Since I could not measure up to other people's expectations, I remained depressed, sat around thinking about my problems, and wondered how I could escape.

I also wanted to succeed at something, but things kept coming against me. I began to feel like I wasn't going to succeed at anything. As a result, this brought on another problem—a low self-image.

At that time, I did not realize that I was basing my acceptance on my performance, or on how I thought people viewed me. Most of my life, I felt like I had to be perfect in order for people to accept me. As a result, I tried another way to escape – I fell asleep.

(2) Sleeping

Sleeping is another way you can use to escape your problems. Your problems can also keep you from getting any sleep.

Let's picture this scene.

You are lying in bed. With your mind focused on your problems, you begin tossing and turning side to side trying to find a comfortable position. Hoping to drift off to sleep soon, you try to relax and close your eyes. However, you are still having trouble sleeping because your mind is focused on your problems. Before you realize it, you fall asleep. You might even have nightmares about something that involves a trial you are going through.

When that happens, you have a restless night. The next day, you are so tired that you have a difficult time functioning. You may drift off to sleep during the day because of your lack of sleep the night before. Is it worth it?

You need to be able to function at your job, so in order to do that, you need to let go of your problems and try to sleep. You cannot get a good night's sleep or accomplish anything by worrying about your frustrations.

My Experience

I have had trouble sleeping at night because of my circumstances. Usually, it was because I have not had enough money to meet my financial obligations. That has been most of my problems. It just did not seem like I could earn enough money to meet my essential needs like utilities, house payments, doctor bills, groceries, and other needs. I could not stand staying awake and thinking about these things. I felt like nobody could or wanted to help me during my difficult circumstances.

I tried to doze off during the day in order to avoid my unhappy thoughts. However, when I woke up, my problems were still there because I had not dealt with them.

At night, I would pray or turn on the television so I could fall asleep. Praying is better than television, but either one worked for me. When I prayed, I fell asleep quickly.

Television also helped me at times. However, there were times when I struggled with my thoughts about my circumstances while I watched television.

(3) Television

Television was another way people use to escape from their problems, or at least they think it might be. Sometimes, you may watch television all day in order to avoid thinking of your trials. As a result, you become so involved in the shows and the characters that other problems soon arise.

First, you may try to watch too much television as a way to escape your problems. However, you may end up seeing a show where the characters are experiencing the same type of problem or problems you are going through.

In a way, that is good because you can see how they are dealing with their problems. On the other hand, you watched television to escape your problems. Now, you are still confronted with your trials. As a result, television did not help you overcome your circumstances.

Second, you may find that you cannot get along without a certain program or programs. You think you have to watch a particular show at that time no matter what else you are doing. When that happens, you are placing the media first in your life. God wants you to place Him first in your life.

Finally, by watching television constantly, you begin to live in a fantasy world instead of dealing with your problems. You think about the characters. You become involved in their lives and believe they are reality. You enjoy watching the shows instead of dealing with your own reality and the trials that you are facing in your life.

However, you need to live in reality and deal with your problems. Your trials will not go away by watching television.

There is nothing wrong in watching television or going to movies, but you need to think about the kinds of shows you watch, the amount of time during the day you watch television, and if it interferes with your daily activities. It is easy to get hooked on watching television, but you need to limit the amount of time you and your children spend watching television during the day. You also shouldn't use it as a way to escape your problems. You still have your problems until you have dealt with them.

My Experience

Before I started watching television, I made sure I had my snacks and pop handy so I wouldn't have to get up during the show. However, during the advertisements, I dashed to the refrigerator or cupboard for more snacks.

In the past, my favorite shows were soap operas. When I was out shopping or running errands, I kept checking my watch to see if it was about time for my favorite soap operas to start. I would rush home so I would not miss my shows. I would always plan my activities around my soap operas. As a result, I was letting the television rule my life, but at that time, I did not realize what was happening. Television seemed to help me relax throughout the day even though I was depressed about my circumstances.

Later on in my life I found out I had two disabilities: ADHD and Persistent Anxieties. A counselor told me that having the television on would help me relax and deal with my disabilities. I had trouble working on the computer or reading without the television. By having it on, I could take breaks from my activities. That helped me with my disabilities.

(4) Eating

Eating is another way that people use to escape their problems. Let's think about this situation:

As you are sitting there watching television. Your mind starts to wander. You begin getting restless. You feel the need to get up and search for something to eat. You go out to the kitchen to look through your refrigerator and your cupboards. You finally find something, so you sit down and eat. As a result, you could develop bad eating habits and gain weight while you are trying to forget your circumstances.

Turning to food to help you when you are nervous, depressed, or frustrated about something is wrong because you are not dealing with your problems. Overeating, eating very little, or not eating the right kind of food will cause other problems, and you are not solving your the trials you are experiencing. Therefore, eating is not a way to escape your problems. It may help you temporarily, but you still have your problems.

My Experience

I enjoyed cooking, but when I was frustrated about something, I wanted something handy to eat. I made sure I had snacks around like cookies, chips, cupcakes, or other quick and easy food I could grab.

When I moved back to my parents' house, I found out that I had hypoglycemia. That was one reason I was glad I had moved back home. My mother could help me during my severe weak spells. Since I was hypoglycemic, I had to eat six small meals a day. When I did not eat or eat at the right time, I became weak and lightheaded. I needed to have something quick so I would not pass out, but I also wanted to avoid thinking of my problems.

(5) Shopping

Going shopping is another way that people use to escape their problems. However, it causes more problems. Going shopping is all right if you need something. God wants us to look nice and to have the things that we need to live and be a witness for Him.

However, if you buy things just to make yourself feel better, you have a problem. You are shopping as a way to escape your unpleasant circumstances instead of dealing with them. You think that going shopping will help you overcome your problems or will help you to feel better, but you are wrong. You are not spending your money wisely, and you are not dealing with your circumstances.

Credit cards can be another problem. It is easy to overspend, and then you have trouble paying off your bills. Some creditors might be willing to work with you, but others harass you over the phone and threaten you.

After you pay off your bills, you still cannot charge again with them because they view you as a bad person. Even though you have established better credit ratings, people do not want to give you another chance. They look at you as a bad person because of your past mistakes.

Everybody has trouble in his/her lives, but if you make mistakes, people are not willing to give you another chance. To me this is wrong. People should help you because people change, but creditors are not willing to help you.

My Experience

In the past, when I was a day care provider, I would go shopping as soon as the last child left. Since I enjoyed reading Mysteries and Crime Fiction, I went to my favorite bookstores so I could browse through that section. I would also search the sections where books were on sale. Sometimes I would find some great bargains. I could also use my purchases as a tax deduction since I was a freelance writer.

I enjoyed reading great mysteries especially from authors like Agatha Christie, Erle Stanley Gardner, Raymond Chandler, and other mystery writers. Since I continued to develop my interest in Mysteries, Crime Fiction, and the subgenres, I wanted to read books by authors who were new to me. If I found an author whom I liked, I would buy just about every book they had written. My bookshelves were getting full. As a result, I had to purchase other bookcases to hold all my books. I also enjoyed reading anthologies because they contained several short stories by different authors. That way, I become familiar with different writers.

Because I was a freelance writer, I wanted office supplies to help me organize my computer area. I went to office supply stores so I could purchase these items. I enjoyed organizing my bookshelves and computer area. I wanted things so that I would know where they were located if I needed to find something quickly. I became upset if I could not find something when I needed it.

Besides bookstores and office supply stores, I went to other stores where I could buy clothes so I could look nice. I did not feel like I was as attractive as other people were, so I wanted to purchase items that helped me feel better as a person.

However, several of these purchases did not last long. I thought these items would make me happy, but after awhile I wanted something else. As a result, I ended up with very little money and things lying around I did not need or use. I continued to feel depressed, lonely, and unhappy with myself as a person. Everything I tried seemed to go wrong. Other people had things and seemed to have their lives together, but not me. I was a failure. I wanted to succeed, but I did not know what I could do in my life.

(6) Sinful Activities

Another way to escape is by going to bars or parties where you might engage in sinful activities such as drugs, sex, alcohol, or other types of inappropriate behavior.

Going to movies that show sex, violence, or bad language, or going to stores where they sell only adult material is not good for your spiritual growth. You should not engage in sinful activities that might arouse your fleshly desires because you would have extra problems. Is it worth it?

(7) Prescription and Non-Prescription Drugs

Taking drugs like cocaine and marijuana will only add to your present frustrations. Drugs will affect you in the following ways:

(1) They can cause emotional swings up or down.

(2) They can kill you or others.

(3) They can harm unborn babies.

(4) You can get arrested.

Whether they are legal or illegal, drugs might make you feel good for a little while. However, they will not solve your problems. Drugs can also cause you to be so tired that all you want to do is sleep instead of dealing with reality.

(8) Alcoholic Beverages

If you drink alcoholic beverages in excessive amounts you will harm yourself as well as others around you, especially if you drive while you are intoxicated. Drinking helps you to forget your problems temporarily, but you still have to deal with them.

My Experience

I never drank alcoholic beverages, but I have known others who have, and I have seen the results. To me, there is no purpose in getting drunk. It does not solve anything. You may have temporarily forgotten your frustrations, but eventually you will remember them unless something happens to you first.

I have seen someone, who was close to me, drive after he had been drinking. Even though nothing happened, it was a scary situation. It is also against the law to drive while intoxicated.

(9) Running Away

Sometimes, you want to move because you want to run away from your present circumstances. You think things will work out better for you in another city or state. If you are running away to avoid your circumstances, you will not be happy. Your problems will follow you no matter where you live or what you do because you have not faced your problems head on and dealt with the root.

My Experience

I moved to Lawrence, instead of staying in Topeka when things frustrated me. Even though I moved because of my frustrations, I wanted to go to Kansas University.

Because I went to Kansas University, I graduated with a BGS Degree in Human Development and Family Life, and that helped me to feel like I succeeded at something.

After I graduated, I started a day care and continued to teach piano. However, in 1982, I had financial problems because I lost my piano students and children in my day care.

As a result, I began to feel like a failure. I kept having negative things happen in my life. My phone bill was also high because I called my mother a lot. We had a close relationship, and I missed being around her, so I decided to move back to Topeka. After I sold my house in Lawrence, I bought a house in Topeka, which was not too far from where my parents lived, so I was happy again.

(10) Suicide

Suicide is a permanent end to all of your problems, but it is not the right way to deal with them. However, some people have taken that route because they have given up and let their problems get the best of them.

My Experience

There were times when I did not want to live and, but if I had taken my life, I would have gone to hell. I also would not have had the opportunity to write this book, so I could share my life with you and to show you how to deal with your circumstances.

Trying to escape will not solve your problems. You need to understand the meaning of life, and then you can deal with your circumstances.

Chapter Nine
Woe Is Me!

Sometimes when you are going through a trial, a past hurt that you are hanging on to may flash before your eyes and cause you to be even more depressed. This happens if something in your life triggers something in your past.

Past Hurts

When I tried to do something, people would tell me that I could not do it, or they would tell me to do it by myself when I did not know what to do. As a result, I became frustrated and depressed. It seemed like people wanted to criticize me instead of helping me. Here are some questions are thoughts that I have had and probably you have, too.

(1) Why am I always criticized? (2) Nobody cares for me. (3) I can't do anything right. (4) Everything I try to do, fails. (5) I wish somebody cared for me. (6) God doesn't care for me. (7) I feel like a failure. (8) Will anything work out for me?

Do these feelings sound familiar? Have you felt like a failure, lonely, depressed, rejected, or had other feelings? I am sure you have. I know that I have had these feelings or questions. These are negative thoughts.

Negative Thinking

When a negative thought appears in your mind, you begin dwelling on that thought. Suddenly, you start believing it, and you develop more negative thoughts. Within a few minutes, you become depressed because of your thoughts. These emotions are a result of past hurts that you have buried in your subconscious mind. When you are going through a trial, a past hurt or a negative thought may flash before your eyes and cause you to be depressed. This happens when something in your present circumstances triggered something in your past. Let's look at these scenes:

Scene 1--Present Scene

"Tina why haven't you been doing your homework?" her mother shouted.

"I don't know."

"I'm not going to put up with these bad grades. All you want to do is play. You're lazy. You don't want to learn."

"That's not true," Tina replied, as tears rolled down her cheeks. "I don't understand my assignments."

"Study harder. I want good grades next time."

"Why are you always yelling and criticizing me?" Tina asked, as she ran to her room.

As Nancy thought about what Tina said, a past memory flashed before her. She remembered an incident of her childhood.

Scene 2--Flashback

"Nancy, clean up this mess! I can't stand it. Your room is always cluttered," her mother shouted, as she left the room.

"Nancy started to clean up her room and then walked downstairs to eat supper.

When Nancy entered the room, she saw her father sitting at the table and her mother standing in front of the counter. "Hi, Daddy," Nancy said, as she sat down.

"Hi, Sweetheart."

"Is your room clean?" her mother asked, as she placed the food on the table.

"Some of it."

"I want it cleaned up before you go to bed."

After supper, Nancy walked upstairs to her room. Within a few minutes, her mother came in and shouted, "This room is still a mess. You have toys under your bed and your shelves are a mess. Can't you do anything? I'm tired of your laziness and your messy room."

Sitting there with tears in her eyes, Nancy burst out crying when her mother left the room. "Why is Mommy always yelling at me? She hates me. I can't do anything right."

Nancy thought about her past and realized how she felt and how Tina must have felt. Nancy's mother treated her the same way Nancy treated her daughter, Tina.

My Experience

I have been hurt by friends, family, teachers, peers, and anyone who was critical of me. Sometimes when I thought about my struggles in the present, past hurts would appear in my mind. I tried to avoid thinking about the past hurts, but he was difficult.

I did not have many friends during the time I was in school. Several peers teased me and made fun of me, which hurt. One girl even got someone to call me up and ask me out. However, she meant it as a joke. Nobody showed up, and that really hurt me. I found out who had played the joke on me, and my mother and I confronted her and her mother. The girl apologized at that time. As a result, I felt nobody really cared for me. I felt like people wanted to mistreat me.

During the time from 1967 to 1977, I attended Washburn University as well as searched for a job. I couldn't take a full load, so it took me awhile. In 1971, I had trouble with my grades, so I could not return to school the next semester. That year, my mother became seriously ill, so I had to take her to the hospital. Since I enjoyed taking care of her, she thought I would like to work in a hospital as a Nurses-Aide.

I tried a Nurses-Aide training, but I could not finish the training because my instructor told me that I was not good around people and that I should work with machines. I did a good job in my course work, but they did not help me to do the physical work. They gave me work that was too difficult for one person to do. As a result, they did not want me to continue my training. I became upset, but I decided to try something different.

The people at the hospital told me I should work with machines because I was not good around people. I decided to enroll in a clerk-typist training. However, that did not work out either. When I graduated, my instructor told me she hoped I never get a job.

As a result, I became upset and was depressed most of the time. I felt like a failure and felt like nobody wanted to help me. I wanted to give up, but for some reason I had the desire to press onward in search of something I could do.

The next semester, I enrolled at Washburn, but I still had trouble. I wanted to give up again because I still felt like I could not do anything. I continued to be depressed with my life. I wanted to be successful, but I wondered what I could do. Everything I tried to do seemed to fail. I gave up going to Washburn since I couldn't succeed there.

Because of my failures, I felt like God seemed far away. If God was around, why did He cause me to fail all the time?

As I already mentioned, I felt like I had to be perfect. If I made a mistake, people turned away. I did not think I was ever going to be good at anything. As a result, I felt rejected and life seemed hopeless. Was there any hope for me? I did not know where to turn. By this time, I developed an unhealthy self-image.

Focusing On Your Circumstances

If you continually focus on your problems during the day or at night, you become so overwhelmed that your frustrations seem bigger than you can handle. As a result, you feel like you cannot do anything because everything seems hopeless. You want to succeed, but everything you attempt to do seems to fail.

Because you feel so overwhelmed with your circumstances, you may seek out different people who will listen to you or sympathize with you. You think that talking to people will help you overcome your trials. Sometimes it does because we need each other for support. However, you cannot depend on others to solve your trials.

You may also become jealous of others who seem to have it all together. You want to be like them. You start to compare yourself to others. You may focus on other people and their material possessions or their abilities and talents because you view them as better than you are. As a result, you view yourself as inadequate.

Material Possessions

As you look at others and dwell on what material possessions they have, then you become jealous of them if you do not have what they have. Eventually, you become angry and discontent with your life and what material possessions you do not have. You start wonder why everything seems to be coming against you. You may even go out and buy something you want that other people have, so you can be equal with them. There is nothing wrong with material possessions, except for the value you place on things.

Abilities and Talents

Comparing yourself to others is another way that you will end up with an unhealthy self-image. You will be depressed because you will not feel as capable of doing things as other people. You have your own special abilities and talents. You need to find out what you can do and strive toward that goal or goals.

My Experience

For as long as I can remember, I wanted to write and have my material published. I also wanted to minister to others through my writing. However, at the time, I felt like that was not going to happen.

In 1992, I had a craft project published. Then, in 1998, I began having several articles, short stories, mini-mysteries, and book reviews published through Suite101.com. I began my own websites through Suite101.com.

That helped developed my self-esteem. On the other hand, I wasn't bringing in the income I needed. I needed to find something that I liked doing where I could meet my financial obligations and that helped build up my self-esteem.

Rejection

When you have felt rejected, you do not have a desire to be close to people. On the other hand, you want to have friends, but you feel like you cannot trust people. You do not want others to reject you again. You want people to love and accept you, but you are afraid of being hurt. You try and hide your past hurts, but your actions reveal that you have not dealt with your feelings.

(1) You may force yourself on people by going to them with your problems.

Sometimes, you may go to someone you feel close to for some advice concerning a problem or problems you have, but if you do not go to them with the motive of doing something about your problem, then you are going with the wrong motive. You just want sympathy or someone to help you through your trials.

If you constantly go to the same person with your problems, that person will eventually turn away from you because of the unhealthy attachment you have formed with that person until the problem is resolved.

(2) You may try to draw attention to yourself through a physical problem or problems.

No matter what problems you may have, if you have constantly felt rejected in the past, you want to have sympathy and attention instead of healing. You believe that if you do not have any problems, then people will not show you love or attention.

(3) Doing good works for others.

There is nothing wrong with doing good works for people, but you need to have the right motive. If you do good things for people so they will accept you, then your motive is not right. You are doing things for people to earn their love, which is wrong.

You may also try to do something good for people if you have felt rejected. You want to feel loved by others so you try to do good deeds for them. It does not help and you begin to feel lonely.

Loneliness

Sometimes you feel lonely when you experience some difficult times. Because of your feelings of loneliness, you try too hard to reach out to others. As a result, people could turn away from you because they feel overwhelmed by your need for so much love and attention. Everyone has experienced loneliness.

If you are lonely, you may want a lot of noise around such as the television, radio, or stereo. You may also talk on the phone too much, so you will not be lonely. Sometimes, if you are lonely you have a tendency to become involved in too many activities. As a result, you do not have time to be by yourself and deal with your inner feelings.

My Experience

I have experienced loneliness several times throughout my life. Even when I was in a crowd of people, I felt lonely. I sat by myself and hoped someone would come over to me. I tried to enter into conversations at times, but I felt like I was intruding. As a result, I stayed by myself most of the time unless someone did come and talk to me.

Pets are another way to cope with loneliness. I have four dogs, and they know me as "Mommy." I have taught them a lot of tricks, and they even know spelling words. They really keep me company when I feel lonely. I enjoy their companionship, and they show me a lot of love and attention, too.

Besides my dogs, I work as an online tutor, freelance writer, piano teacher, and a substitute teacher. I enjoy my life because I have a variety of things to do.

How to cope with loneliness

The most important way to cope with loneliness is to accept Christ as your Savior and spend time with God everyday. You will learn more about this in a later chapter.

You can keep yourself too busy because you feel lonely. You need to decide which activities you would like to do and give up the other activities that you feel are not as important.

You also need to find ways that will help you to not feel so lonely. If you are a parent, spending time with your children is very important for you and for them. If you are not a parent (like me), then you need to look for other ways to occupy your time such as having friends over, pets, or going to work.

If you work away from home, your may experience some lonely times when you go home, especially if you are single. To help you overcome your loneliness, you need to think about doing things like craft projects, writing, listening to music, watching the television, going to a movie, spending time eating out, reading, or relaxing.

You have a choice to make. You can hang onto your loneliness or other past hurts, or you can deal with them. Hanging onto your past hurts means burying them in your subconscious mind and then hoping you will forget them.

Dealing with your past hurts means you have decided to be free from all anger, bitterness, hatred, resentment, unforgiveness, and other feelings cause you to develop an unhealthy self-image.

Self-Image

Your self-image is how you view yourself and what you base your self-image on. If you are not sure of your opinion, ask yourself this question: "Who am I?" How you answer that question will be the basis of your self-image. Let's take a closer look at the difference between an unhealthy self-image and a healthy self-image.

Unhealthy Self-Image

You are probably most familiar with the terms low self-image or poor self-image. I prefer to use the term unhealthy self-image because you will be unhealthy physically, emotionally, spiritually, and mentally if you base your self-image on any of the following: (1) Occupation (2) Finances or Material Possessions (3) Good Works (4) People (5) Marriage or Sex (6) Drugs, Alcohol, or Smoking.

(1) Occupation

If you see yourself as a mother (father), housewife (husband), teacher, writer, doctor, lawyer, sales clerk, or other types of occupations; you are viewing yourself on what you do and not on you as a person. You will talk to people about their work instead of getting to know them in a personal way.

For example, if you have a personal friendship with your doctor and all you do is talk to him about medicine when he is off work, then you will not get to know him personally. Doctors, teachers, lawyers, or other professional people, all need a break in the evening when they get off work unless it is an emergency. Focus your time on getting to know how people feel and their opinions about other topics such as hobbies, interests, goals in life, or other personal feelings.

Leave work at work.

However, this is hard to do if you work at home. You need to have a separate room, if possible, in your house for work so that in the evening you can shut the door and go to another part of your house to do your household activities or just relax.

When you work at home, your hours are flexible. You can set up certain hours that you will work and discuss work during that time. The important thing to remember is to allow yourself some time with your family, friends, or yourself so you can relax.

My Experience

Since I worked at home, it was difficult to find time to relax or get away from work. I first started out as a piano teacher and taught at my house. After I graduated from Kansas University, I became a day care provider and continued teaching piano.

When I lived in Lawrence, I had the weekends off, which gave me time to come back to Topeka to see my parents. Then, I returned to Lawrence on Sunday.

(2) Finances or Material Possessions

Sometimes, you may want to have the best job available so you can live in an expensive house and drive expensive vehicles. Having these things might make you happy and feel good about yourself, but how would you feel if you lost everything? Would you feel angry? Would you feel like a failure? Your self-image would be unsteady and insecure if you placed too much value on these things.

There is nothing wrong in having a good job, material possessions, or success unless you base your self-image on these things. If you are, then you need to change your attitude or get rid of some the things that you value too high in your life.

My Experience

As I mentioned before, I could not afford to stay in Lawrence, so I bought a house in Topeka. I started a day care in my home and taught piano again. However, in August 1992, I lost my house and had to move back home with my parents, which devastated me at the time.

(3) Good Works

If others have rejected you, or you have felt they have rejected you, then you will most likely feel rejected by God. As a result, you will develop a low opinion of yourself.

You want others to accept you, but you have a hard time trusting people or God. You feel that if you made a mistake, people would turn away from you. As a result, you may try to build up your self-image by doing good things for others or for God so people or God will accept you.

My Experience

Most of my life, I based my self-image on my performance. If I did well, people gave me a reward. If I made a mistake, people turned away from me or criticized my abilities. Sometimes, people did not give me another chance to show them I could change.

When I was not sure of what to do in certain situations, I asked for some help, but people would not help me. They told me I knew what to do and that I was to figure it out myself. I became so frustrated when I could not figure things out that I just gave up. Sometimes, I ran off by myself and cried.

As a day care provider and a piano teacher, I felt like I had to be perfect or people would stop my services. If I made one mistake, people would terminate my services. If they had discussed the situation, things might have worked out.

(4) People

Sometimes, if you are close to someone, you might pattern your life after that person. For example, you may dress like them, talk like them, act like them, or do the same kind of job they do so you will have a better self-image.

If you have had an unhealthy self-image, then you may feel like you cannot do things on your own. As a result, you try and depend on others to help you work through your problems or the things that you think you cannot do by yourself.

My Experience

In the past, I had friends who wanted to do the same kind of job I did. If I changed jobs, then they would, too. I always wondered why they did that, but as I thought about it, I began to feel like they were jealous of me. They did not want to develop their own abilities.

If I felt like I could not do things on my own, I tried to depend on others to help me. I found out that if I constantly depended on someone to help me with my problems, then they would leave me, which made me feel rejected.

(5) Marriage or Sex

If you are single, you might be telling yourself the following: (1) "If only I were married, then I would be happy." (2) "If only I were married like all of my friends, then I would feel good about myself." (3) "If only men could show me love, then I'd be happy."

Getting married or wanting sexual relationships is not completely satisfying. You still have trials. You need to be happy and satisfied in the relationships you have. If you are to be married, then it will work out.

(6) Drugs, Alcohol, and Smoking

Teenagers use drugs because they get involved with the wrong crowd, either by accident or on purpose. Teenagers, who have a lot of emotional problems, want someone to help them overcome their frustrations. As a result, they turn to friends, who may in turn lead them to a drug pusher. Suddenly, they start on the drug scene. After a few "highs", teenagers continue on their drug habit and shortly become so dependent on drugs that they begin to steal or do anything they can to support their habit.

If you look to drugs to build a healthy self-image, what happens when you do not have any money for drugs? How would you feel when the drugs start to wear off? What happens to your self-image, then? Drugs, alcohol, and smoking may cause good feelings as well as cause you to forget your problems temporarily, but if you overdose on drugs or alcohol, they can kill you or others. Smoking can also harm you and others physically as well as kill you because it causes cancer.

Non-smokers do not want to be in a smoke filled environment. Some non-smokers are allergic to smoke. If you have to smoke, then I feel you should do it in your own home and not around others who cannot stand your smoke. However, if you smoke in your own home and people come to visit you, you should be polite enough to ask them if your smoking causes them a problem. Because smoke is so strong, people who do not smoke or who are allergic to smoke can smell the odor even if you are not smoking at that particular time. Make sure your home is odor free in case someone stops by.

My Experience

I do not smoke because I am highly allergic to smoke, and I have asthma. People do not have to be smoking at the time for others to have reactions to smoking. When I am shopping and people pass me in the aisles or stand in the checkout lines, I can smell the odor on their clothes. As a result, I end up with an asthma attack. I have to stop where I am and use my inhaler. Second hand smoke is harmful to others. Therefore, smokers should be considerate of others. I have also had trouble even entering a building because smokers have to stand by the door and smoke. This caused me problems before I even started shopping.

Chapter Ten
Searching For Acceptance

You want others to accept you. If you have felt lonely, rejected, or like a failure, you start to believe there is something wrong with you. You feel like nobody cares for you. You probably have asked yourself this question: "Does anyone care?"

Does Anyone Care?

If you have asked yourself that question, then you probably have tried searching for love and acceptance through any of these various ways: Drugs, Alcohol, Socialization, Outward Appearance, Religion, Past Hurts, and Good Works.

(1) Drugs and Alcohol

If you are lonely and want to be accepted, you might become involved in drugs and/or alcohol. By hanging out in bars in order to find acceptance, you will get involved with the wrong kind of people. Drinking and drugs cause all kinds of trouble physically, mentally, emotionally, and spiritually.

Drinking or taking drugs is not the way to be accepted. People will accept you for what you are doing and not for who you really are.

(2) Socialization

Having people over is another way you may try to gain acceptance. You may think will not be lonely if you are around people. However, socializing does not solve your loneliness. You can be with a group of people and still feel lonely inside.

For example, if you are at a family gathering or a social event and you are standing around with nobody to talk to, then you can feel lonely. Even if you are near someone and other people are talking, you can still feel lonely. You have to take the initiative and enter into the conversation by listening to others, or by speaking up when you feel led to talk.

Sometimes, if you do not feel accepted, or if you have other emotional problems, you may go shopping for new clothes so you can feel better. You need a variety of clothes, but you do not need to buy something new everyday. You may also buy makeup and jewelry to feel better about your appearance. There is nothing wrong in wearing makeup and jewelry except for the amount of makeup or jewelry you wear.

I have seen some women wear a lot of jewelry or makeup. Your makeup should be according to your skin color and hair color. It is important to choose colors that look best on you, and you should use it sparingly. When you use an excessive amount of makeup or jewelry, you are drawing attention to yourself.

(3) Religion

Getting involved in religion is another way you may use to find acceptance. If you decide that religion is the way to find acceptance, you may try a religious groups, or attend several churches.

If you attend church to find acceptance or to do something good for someone, then your motives are wrong. Good works is not the way to earn acceptance or to go to heaven.

(4) Past Hurts

If you have not dealt with your past hurts, you may dwell on those hurts. They will affect your life and your relationship with others. For example, I mentioned that several people criticized me throughout my life. As a result, I had trouble dealing with criticism. You need to think about what people say to you, and if you feel like their comments are helpful, then you need to do something about it. If you feel like the comments are negative and people are cutting you down personally, then you need to let those comments go.

Realize you are human and that you do make mistakes. You need to learn from your mistakes, instead of letting people's negative comments rule your life. Dwelling on your past hurts can affect your circumstances and relationships. Let go of your past hurts and press onward.

(5) Good Works

Doing good works is another way to find acceptance. People will accept you for who you are and not for what you do for them.

If you have felt rejected throughout your life, you have probably based your acceptance on your performance. If you received a reward for doing good works, you probably felt accepted. If you were criticized for not making good grades or doing something wrong, then you probably felt rejected because you have not lived up to other people's expectations. When that happens, you base your acceptance on your performance.

My Dream

A few weeks later, I had a dream about God and Satan. I dreamed that I was down in hell and every time I did something good, I could move up closer to heaven. When I shared this with Dick, he told me I still believed I had to earn salvation. I left feeling confused and not sure about my salvation. However, I felt like Dick told me the truth about my life. I continued going to church and to Bible studies.

I felt God loved me if I did good things, and if I did not do something right, I felt like He did not love me. I also felt that if something went wrong in my life such as burning something I was cooking, I felt like God did not care about me. I felt like things had to be perfect in my life in order for God to love me or to accept me.

Throughout my life, I wanted to be loved and accepted by people, but I felt I had to be perfect in order for people to love and accept me. I was not perfect and had trouble doing good things, so I felt like nobody cared or accepted me, but I did not know how to resolve my problems. I wanted to be accepted.

Chapter Eleven
The Missing Link

If you feel like something is missing in your life or that God seems far away, your relationship or your fellowship with God may not be right. You need to find out what the missing link is in your life and deal with it. It could be one of the following:

       (1)   You have not been born again.

       (2)   You have backslid.

       (3)   You believe in things that are not Biblical.

Head or Heart Knowledge

Knowing about God and knowing Him personally are two different aspects. Learning about God is developing a head knowledge. By reading the Bible, you will know the facts about God, but you will not know God intimately. Knowing God in a personal way is developing a relationship with Him.

Head Knowledge (Knowing About God)

Learning about God is finding out the facts about Him. It is like trying to find out more information about some famous movie star or other famous person whom you have not met personally.

Children who write school reports about a famous person will read books or encyclopedias to gather up information for their reports. They do not know how the person feels or thinks about things. When you gather facts about someone, you are developing a head knowledge about that person.

If you want to learn about God, you would read the Bible and go to church, but having a head knowledge is not the way to eternal life. There are a lot of people in this world who think they are going to heaven, but they need genuine relationship with God.

You may go to church for motives other than developing a personal relationship with God. You may or may not listen or become involved in the service. You may go to church and learn about God, but when you go home, you continue to live your life the way you had been. You may also think that going to church and being around people will help solve their loneliness, but it does not help. You can still be in church and feel lonely inside. You have not dealt with your feelings of loneliness. You believe that if you are around a group of people that you will not be lonely, but you will.

You may also go to different churches seeking acceptance. If you do not feel accepted at one church, you will go to another church until you find one where you eel accepted.

On the other hand, you may go to church only on Christmas and Easter because you believe it is the thing to do. However, your reason for going to church should be to know God in a personal way and to develop a relationship with Him.

Relationship

Relationship means being related to someone. For example, you are related to your mother and father, or brothers and sisters, and other relatives. That relationship will not be broken.

Relationship With God

God is your heavenly Father if you have accepted Jesus as your Savior and Lord. That relationship will not be broken even if you sin. God will never leave you. God created you and wants to have a relationship with you. Because sin entered the world, the relationship between God and man was broken. Jesus died so that the relationship between God and man would be restored.

Heart Knowledge (Personal Relationship)

Reading the Bible helps you to find out facts about God, but you will not know Him personally unless you spend time getting to know Him as a person. Just like you have developed a relationship with your earthly father, God wants you to know Him. He is your heavenly Father. You need to know how He reacts to different situations, feelings, beliefs, and other characteristics. God wants to speak to you and the only way to know His voice is by spending time with Him. If you did not spend time with God, you would not be able to discern whether you were hearing His voice, Satan□s voice, or your thoughts.

You spend time with people in order to recognize their voices. For example, if you have spent time getting to know someone, you would be able to recognize that person□s voice on the phone. You can know God personally by spending time with Him. However, before you can develop a relationship with Him, you need to accept Jesus as your Savior.

Relationship Without God

God is not your Father if you have not accepted Jesus as your Savior and Lord. If you prayed with motives other than wanting to develop a personal relationship with Jesus, or you have tried to earn salvation by being good, you do not have a relationship with God. Jesus is the way to salvation. You cannot earn salvation or by being religious.

My Experience

In the past, I learned the facts about God, but I did not develop a personal relationship with Him. I read my Bible, went to Bible studies, went to church, and claimed to be a Christian because I prayed. However, I finally found the missing link.

Chapter Twelve
Where's Your Destination?

God wants you to make a decision about your destination. In Matthew 7:13-14, there are two paths to take. One is through the narrow gate, and one is through the wide gate. Where is your destination? Is it through the narrow gate or through the wide gate?

(13)   *Enter through the narrow gate.*
       For wide is the age and broad
       is the road that leads to destruction,
       and many enter through it

(14)   *But small is the gate and narrow the road that*
       leads to life, and only a few find it.
       (Matthew 7:13-14)

God's Plan

I enjoy reading and writing mysteries and the subgenres. One day, I realized that life was like an exciting mystery because you never know what to expect in the future. God knows what is best for you and wants to develop a personal relationship with you, so He can have fellowship with you and reveal His plan for your life. He wants you to spend time reading His Word daily, meditating on it, memorizing it, and praying for His guidance for your life. Jeremiah 29:11 shows you that God has good plans for you and that He does not want to harm you.

> (11)   *"For I know the plans I have for you,"*
> *declares the Lord, "plans to prosper*
> *you and not to harm you, plans to*
> *give you hope and a future."*
> (Jeremiah 29:11)

The narrow gate leads to the path of life, so if you want life, then you need to follow God's plan. Remember, that He has plans for you to prosper and does not want to harm you. However, all of us want to make our own decisions in life as to what we want to do.

Your Plan

When you take your life into your own hands and make all of your decisions, then you will end up on the wide path, which leads to destruction. God created you and has a plan for your life. You may decide to go off to some foreign country and be a missionary, but God may want you to minister to people in your own country. You may not even have a desire to follow God and may end up follow different cult groups, which could harm you physically and emotionally. Even though your plans may seem great and not harmful, without God, your life will lead to destruction. However, you do have a choice to make.

You can choose to follow God and have a life of prosperity, or you can choose to follow your own desires and have a life of destruction. Who knows, maybe what you desire to do in life, could be God's plan for you, but without God, you will not prosper.

Life or Death

If you want to live a life with God, all you have to do is agree with God about your sin. The following verses show you that everyone has sinned and that sin results in death.

> (23) *"For all have sinned and fall short*
> *of the glory of God,*
> (Romans 3:23)

> (23) *"For the wages of sin is death, but the gift*
> of God is eternal life in Christ Jesus our Lord."
> (Romans 6:23)

After you have acknowledged that you are sinner and that sin results in death, then you need to decide if you want to repent of your sins, which is making a decision to turn from your sins and turn to God. God gives you life and freedom from sin and death because He loves you.

God's Love and Acceptance

Jesus loved you so much that He died for your sins. Even if you were the only one around, He would have still died for you because He loves you and accepts you as you are. No matter what you have done, you can come to God and know that He will forgive you and cleanse you of all of your sins. He also forgets every sin you have committed.

Knowing this fact should give you the desire to turn to Him. All you have to do is to accept His love and forgiveness.

(8)   *"But God demonstrates his own love for us in this: While we were still sinners, Christ died for us."* (Romans 5:8)

(16)   *"For God so loved the world that he gave his one and only Son, that whoever believes in him shall not perish but have eternal life."* (John 3:16)

Knowing God Personally

In order to know God personally, you need to accept Him as Savior and Lord. He created you for fellowship with Him. In the beginning, there was no sickness, death, or sin. Everything was perfect.

When Adam and Eve ate from the tree of the Knowledge of Good and Evil, they gave into their fleshly desires and turned from God and what He wanted for their lives. God created you for a purpose. If you follow these easy steps to salvation, you will be able to seek after God and find out what your purpose is in life. You will be glad you did.

However, you need to make an important decision about your life. You can choose to hang on to your sins and live according to your fleshly desires, or you can choose to repent, which means turning away from your sins and turning to God. Repentance leads to eternal life. If you are not sure about repenting of your sins, then you need to keep reading. If you have repented of your sins and have accepted Christ as your Savior and Lord, you can still review the steps of Salvation.

Steps of Salvation

Step One - Repentance

Repentance means to turn away from sin and turn to God. God created you for fellowship with Him and He wants you to accept His love.

You need to agree with God on the following things:

(1)   You are a sinner, and you will have eternal death.

(2)   He loves you. He created you for a purpose.

(3)   He died for you, so that you will not suffer eternal death.

(4)   He rose for you so that you will have a victorious life.

When you have that settled in your heart, then you need to make a decision to turn to God. After you have repented of your sins, then you need to confess your sins to God and ask Him to forgive you of your sins.

Repentance is making a decision to turn completely away from anything that stands in the way of your relationship with God. It could be drugs, smoking, alcohol, sex, watching television too much, finances, relationships or anything else that you place ahead of God. He wants you to make a decision to follow Him no matter what He asks you to do.

God knows what is best for your life, and He will not harm you because He created you. Think of something you have created--a baby for instance. You want the best for your child. You do not want anything to harm your child. You know what is best for your child, and you will do what you can to protect him or her. That is the same way with God. God loves you and wants the best for your life. He wants you to turn to Him and seek His plan for your life.

Step Two - Confession

Confession means to agree with God about your sins. You also need to see how your sins have hurt Him. God wants you to confess your sins and ask Him to forgive you.

God wants you to confess your sins, repent, and ask Him to forgive you. He will forgive you, if you believe Him. Do you believe Him? Have you ever confessed your sins and repented of them? He is waiting right now for you to repent of your sins and turn to Him so that He can cleanse you of your sins. He wants to fellowship with you.

> (9)   *"If we confess our sins, he is faithful*
> *and just and will forgive us our sins*
> *and purify us from all   unrighteousness."*
> (1 John 1:9)

Step Three - Believing

You must believe that Jesus is God and that He came to save you from your sins. If you believe that, then you need to ask Jesus to come into your heart and to cleanse you and to be Savior and Lord of your life. (John 1:12)

If you doubt, you will be tossed to and fro like the waves of the sea. God wants you to believe Him, and He wants you to believe in what He has done on the cross for you.

Step Four - Assurance

You can know for sure that Jesus is in your life.

(11)   *"And this is the testimony:*
        God has given us eternal life,
        and this life is in his Son.

(12)   *He who has the Son has life;*
        he who does not have the Son
        of God does not have life.

(13)   *I write these things to you who*
        believe in the name of the Son
        of God so that you may know
        that you have eternal life."

(1 John 5:11-13)

After you have accepted Christ as your Savior and you know He is with you, Satan will try and cause you to doubt your salvation. When he does, you must cling to the Scripture verse mentioned above. However, if you have not accepted Christ as your Savior, God can still draw you by His Spirit. He will show you if you have truly believed in your heart.

Satan wants to condemn you and make you feel guilty, but God convicts you of sin so that you will turn to Him.

Condemnation

Condemnation is when Satan makes you feel guilty of the sins you have committed against God. He wants to make you feel bad, so that you will be ineffective for God.

(8)   *"Control yourselves and be careful!*
        The devil, your enemy, goes around like a
        roaring lion looking for someone to eat."
        (1 Peter 5:8)

Satan wants to keep you from having a personal relationship with God. He will come at you through your weakest areas and cause you to sin.

My Experience

I have seen Satan come against me and cause me to turn from God. I have also seen him seek after and destroy two of my friends and their marriages. They were both Christians and because of their sinful desires of other mates, they destroyed their marriages and their walk with God. It not only hurt the families involved, but it hurt their friends and their reputation.

A girl friend was murdered because of her husband's actions. Her husband was charged and convicted of the murder. He lost his wife and his children as well as a lot of friends. He is spending his life in prison because of his actions and desires for other relationships. The other friend was divorced, remarried, and lost a lot of friends and family. Satan will come to seek and destroy people so they will turn away from God.

Conviction

God sent the Holy Spirit to live inside you, so that He can guide you in the way He wants you to go. The Holy Spirit also convicts you of sin when you disobey God. The Holy Spirit is grieved when you have sinned. An uneasy feeling comes upon you when you have done something wrong or you are about to do something wrong. The Holy Spirit shows you your sin so that you can repent and make things right with God.

God wants to help you grow, so the Holy Spirit guides you in the direction He wants you to go. When you go astray, you have the Holy Spirit there to put you on the right path again. He wants you to repent of your sins and to change your way of living.

The Holy Spirit also comforts you and brings Bible verses to your mind when you need them for comfort as well as when you are witnessing to others. However, in order for Him to do that, you will need to do your part, which is reading, meditating on and memorizing the Word of God. You will have joy in your life when you develop a daily quiet time with God.

(2)   *"But his delight is in the law*
of the Lord, and on his law he
meditates day and night."
(Psalm 1:2)

By meditating on and memorizing the Word of God, you will be able to stand firm against Satan, and you will not sin against God.

(7)   *"Submit yourselves, then to God.*
Resist the devil, and he will flee
from you."
(James 4:7)

(11)   *"I have hidden your word in my heart*
that I might not sin against you."
(Psalm 119:11)

Spending time with God everyday is important because you need to know God on a personal basis. You can know God personally and develop a personal relationship with Him like you would with anyone else. Some days you might not feel like spending time with God, but you need to do what God commands you to do whether you feel like it or not.

If you have verses memorized, you will be able to stand firm against Satan's attacks. You need to know God's voice, so that you will be able to distinguish between God's voice, Satan's subtle thoughts, and your thoughts.

When you hear something in your spirit, then you need to check it out with God's Word to see if what you heard lines up with God's Word. If it does not line up, then you are not to follow what you heard because it is your thoughts or Satan's attack on your mind.

God loves you and wants to spend time with you. He will lead and guide you in the direction He wants you to go because He created you to have fellowship with Him.

Chapter Thirteen
Accepted Forever

When you accepted Christ as your Savior, you came to Him by faith. Now, you need to live by faith and trust God to help you through your circumstances. No matter what you are going through, God will work things out for your good if you follow His plan and purpose for your life. In order to know God's will, you need to develop a personal relationship with God.

Wow! A Personal Relationship With God

Imagine having a personal relationship with God, the Creator of the Universe. You can know Him like you can anyone else. (1) Praying, (2) Reading the Bible, and (3) Going to church are ways you can develop a personal relationship with God.

(1) Praying

You talk with God like you can anyone else. The only difference is faith. Since you cannot see God, you come to Him by faith. That is, you believe that what God says in His Word is true. For example, He says in Hebrews 13:5, that He will never leave you nor forsake you.

He will always be there for you. When you seek God you can have the assurance that He will be there waiting for you. You can talk to God about anything on your heart because He already knows what you desire before you ask. By spending time with God, you can know Him and His will for your life.

(2) Reading the Bible

Reading and studying the Bible is important for your spiritual growth. The Bible is God's Word to you. In His Word, He will lead and guide you in the direction He wants you to go. God wants you to spend time reading His Word every day.

Besides reading, God wants you to meditate daily on His Word. Meditating is thinking about a certain verse or passage and what God is trying to show you. He also wants you to apply what you learn through His Word. As you ponder over God's Word, you need to ask Him to reveal His will to you and how to apply it to your life. **Remember: God loves you and wants good things for you. Satan wants to destroy you.**

If you let your mind feed on negative thoughts, you are giving room for Satan to move into your life and take control.

Memorizing Scripture is a commandment of God. He wants you to hide His Word in your heart. By memorizing Scripture, you'll have verses ready when you need them.

> *(11)   "Thy Word have I hidden in my heart*
> *that I might now sin against thee."*
> (Psalm 119:11)

You will also grow in your Christian walk by going to church and hearing the Word of God. Fellowship with other Christians is very important.

(3) Going to Church

It is important to find the right church. God will lead you in the direction He wants you to go. God has led me to various churches. Each church that I had attended, I had to leave after a few years because of various reasons. During the spring of 1996, I had started to turn away from God. On June 30, 1996, God led me to another church. There was a play at the church. After the play, I went forward and rededicated my life to God. Someone I met that night encouraged me to go forward. I was glad he did.

You need other Christians for encouragement and so that you can encourage them. Faith comes by hearing the Word of God. Without faith, it is impossible to please God. If you put your faith in God, He will reward you.

> (6) *And without faith it is impossible*
> *to please Him for he who comes*
> *to God must believe that He is,*
> *and that He is a rewarder of those*
> *who seek Him.*
> (Hebrews 11:6)

Without Christian fellowship, you can become discouraged and give Satan more ground to attack you spiritually. God wants you to fellowship with others and learn more about Him. Satan is on the prowl and wants to attack you so you will turn away from God.

God's Discipline

First, you need to ask God to lead and guide you by his Holy Spirit as to what He wants you to do. Go to God in prayer about any desires you have and ask Him to meet your desires if it is His will or ask Him to change your heart if He shows you something different for your life.

Sometimes this is hard to do because you do not know what God's plan is for you. However, always remember that whatever He asks you to do because it is for your best just like it is when you ask your children to do something that is in their best interest. God deals with you like you would or should with your children--out of love.

I hard a time dealing with God's purpose and love for me in 1991 because I always wanted to work at home and take care of my pets.

I began to have more financial trouble and wondered if I should give up my day care and do something else. In November, when things started getting worse for me, I cried out to God for help. I prayed and asked God to show me what to do. Immediately, He spoke to me about being a full-time freelance writer. I was excited because I always wanted to be a writer. After that, I prayed for guidance. God showed me that He wanted me to contact some publishers and ask them for their guidelines.

The next day, I looked in my Writer's Digest Market book and found several publishers. I wrote to them and asked them to send me their guidelines.

Within a week, I started to receive them. Glancing through the material, I noticed that *Together Time* wanted a "Thank You Poster". As I prayed and asked God to show me what to do, He gave me the idea for a "Thank You Calendar." When I completed it, I sent it off and hoped that it would be published.

Finally, in March 1992, they called me and said they wanted to publish it. I was so excited because this was my first project to be published. I enjoyed writing and knew that God would help me get more things published.

Even though I was excited about getting something published, during the time from April 1992 to November 1992, I began to wonder if I could trust God. Everything seemed to go wrong. I was not sure what was going to happen to me.

Since I was not spending time with God like I should have, I felt like He was far away. I was not sure what His plan was for me, but somehow I decided to press onward to find my purpose in life.

In April, my church joined two other churches to become one church. At first, I did not want to go to the new church because it was farther away, and it was going to be bigger than other churches I had attended. However, after I started going, I wanted to stay because I met a few people and felt accepted. I also felt like my spiritual life was working out.

However, my finances continued to remain in a mess. I was down to five children in my day care. Three of them were stopping at the end of May. I also did not have many piano students. In April, I began selling Avon and Melaleuca, but I still did not make enough income to pay my bills. I was a year and a half behind on my house payments and felt discouraged because things were not working out for me financially.

At the end of May, I lost my favorite ring, and on June 2, the people who sold me my house told me to sell it, or they would evict me.

During the summer, I tried to sell my house. I only had one child in my day care, so I did not know what was going to happen to me. Continuing to remain depressed, I did not turn to God because I was angry at Him for allowing this to happen to me.

At the end of June, JoAnn, Ken's wife passed away. This really upset me. It seemed like everything was going wrong in my life.

I felt close to JoAnn and did not know what I would do without her. She was one person I could turn to when I was upset about something, or if I had something exciting to share with her. After her death, I became even more depressed because I loved her so much and would miss her.

By the beginning of September, I had not sold my house, so the owners evicted me at the end of the second week. I remained upset and depressed because a couple of times I thought I had the house sold, but it failed both times. I never found another place of my own, so I had to move back home with my parents. That was the last thing I wanted to do because I had been on my own for fourteen years. I felt like I failed because nothing seemed to work out for me. I continued to wonder what God's plan was for me.

Chapter Fourteen
Fellowship With God

Fellowship means spending time with other people and getting to know them personally. It also means spending time with God. If you have a relationship with God and you are assured of that, then you can have fellowship with God and with others. However, fellowship with God and others can be broken.

Ways Fellowship Can Be Broken
(1) Sin in your life that you have not dealt with

If you have sin in your life that you have not dealt with, then your fellowship with God has been broken until you have confessed your sin. You will also put a strain on the relationship you have with others if you are harboring bitterness, anger, jealousy, unforgiveness, or other unhealthy feelings towards a person.

For example, if you were told to do something and you refused to do it, then your fellowship with that person would be strained. They would not want to be around you.

In order to restore your fellowship, you need to go to whomever you have something against and confess those feelings.

It is like this with God. If you have sin in your life and you knew you needed to ask God to forgive you, then you need to do it so your fellowship with God can be restored. You did not lose your relationship with God when you have sin in your life. You did lose your fellowship with Him until you confess your sin and ask God to forgive you.

(2) Lack of fellowship

You need to spend time with God so you can continue your fellowship with Him. If you did not continue your quiet time with God on a daily basis, or if you had sin in your life, you would not be close to Him. God cannot reveal Himself to you if you do not fellowship with Him on a daily basis.

In order to grow spiritually, you also need to have fellowship with other Christians. You can minister to each other through praying, reading the Bible, and getting to know each other personally. Also, you will be able to identify with each other because others experience some of the things that you are experiencing.

(3) Placing things ahead of God

If you hold onto things and God tells you to give them up and you do not do what he wants you to do, then you are placing too much emphasis on those things. These things can be material possessions people, or some kind of sin. God wants to be first in your life.

God wants your relationship and fellowship with Him and with others to be right. He loves you and accepts you just as you are. Even if you sin, He still loves you.

Accepting Christ does not make your life perfect at that moment. You still have to spend time with God and obey what He shows you. Good works are a result of salvation. They are not the pathway to heaven.

Past Hurts – Letting Go

You can hang onto your past hurts, or you can deal with them. Hanging onto your past hurts means burying them in your subconscious mind and then hoping you will forget them. Sometimes hanging on to your past hurts can be more comforting because you don't have to deal with them.

Dealing with your past hurts means you have made a major decision in your life--to be free from all anger, bitterness, hatred, resentment, unforgiveness, and other feelings. That means you need to confess your hurts and forgive each person who had hurt you in the past. However, you need to be right with God in order to confess your hurts. If you have confessed your sins and asked Jesus into your heart to be your Savior and Lord, then you can deal with your past hurts and ask forgiveness from those who have hurt you.

Satan wants you to harbor these things because he wants you to turn away from God. How you handle your past hurts will determine how you view yourself.

If you constantly depend on one person, or more than one, people will get tired of hearing your problems day after day especially when they try to advise you and you do not do anything to change your situation. People want to help, but you have to be willing to change. Sometimes, you may feel rejected or feel like nobody cares when people turn away from you, but they are not rejecting you. All they want is for you to follow God.

God wants you to deal with your past hurts. By carrying around your past hurts, you have not forgiven the people who have hurt you. Your unforgiveness results in sin because God commands you to forgive those who have hurt you. Then, He will forgive you.

> (13) *Bear with each other and forgive whatever*
> *grievances you may have against one*
> *another. Forgive as the Lord forgave you.*
> (Colossians 3:13)

God also wants you to forget your past and press on to know Him. If you continue to hold grudges, God cannot use you effectively until your sin is dealt with. Holding onto your past will cause you physical problems as well as emotional and spiritual problems. The following verses show you how to deal with your past. You are to forget your past and focus on knowing God in a personal way.

> (13) *Brothers, I do not consider myself*
> *yet to have taken hold of it. But*
> *one thing I do: Forgetting what*
> *is behind and straining toward*
> *what is ahead,*
> (14) *I press on toward the goal to*
> *win the prize for which God*
> *has called me heavenward in Christ Jesus.*
> (Philippians 3:13-14)

If you constantly think about the past, you will be ineffective in dealing with your present circumstances, and your focus will be on yourself and not on God. The past is gone and cannot be changed, but you can change how you live in the present and what you will do in the future.

Chapter Fifteen
Giving Up Or Pressing Onward

Giving up or pressing onward are the two choices that you can make concerning your struggles in life. If you choose to give up by using one or more of the temporary ways to escape or by taking your life, then you are headed for destruction.

If you choose to press onward in life and accept Christ as your Savior (if you have not already), then you need to press onward to know God in a personal way. As you develop your relationship with God, you will know what His will is for your life.

Setting Up Personal Goals

First Goal--Your first goal is to set up a time during the day that you can spend time with God. You should spend time with God everyday and at a specific time if possible. It should be a time when you are alert and distracted by interruptions. God is jealous and wants to be first in your life.

During your Quiet Time with God, Satan will try to distract you. Since he does not want you to spend time with God and develop a close relationship with Him, he will fill your mind with thoughts about your activities for the day or any problems you are going through. You need to take those thoughts captive and resist Satan. Do not allow Satan to steal your quiet time. Second Corinthians 10:5 shows us this fact.

> (5) *We are destroying speculations and every*
>   *lofty thing raised up against the knowledge of*
>   *God, and we are taking every thought captive to*
>   *the obedience of Christ.*
>
> (2 Corinthians 10:5)

Second Goal--You need to have a plan on developing your quiet time. Your plan should involve the following things.

Praying--Prayer is talking with God. He created you for fellowship with Him and wants to communicate with you. You need to pray for others and then for yourself.

Reading--Reading and studying the Bible is important for your spiritual growth. The Bible is God's Word to you. In His Word He will lead and guide you in the direction He wants you to go.

Meditating--Meditating on God's Word is important for your spiritual growth. When you are quiet before God and are thinking about His Word, He will speak to you and show you what He wants you.

Asking--Ask God to help you to apply what you have learned in His Word.

Memorizing--Memorizing Scripture is a commandment of God. He wants you to hide His Word in your heart, so you will have verses ready when you need them for ministering to others or rebuking Satan.

Worshiping--God wants you to worship and praise Him for who He is.

Thanking--God wants you to thank Him for the things He has done in your life and your prayer needs. When you pray for things, He wants you to believe that you have received your answers and start thanking Him for your prayer needs.

Believing--Faith pleases God. He wants you to believe that He will do what He says He will do. God is not a liar. Satan will try to deceive you because he is the Father of Lies. God wants you to trust Him and to put your faith in God and in His Word.

> (6)   *And without faith it is impossible*
>   *to please Him, for he who comes*
>   *to God must believe that He is,*
>   *and that He is a rewarder of*
>   *those who seek Him.*
>   (Hebrews 11:6)

Third Goal--At the end of your Quiet Time, you need to write down prayer needs for others and yourself, memory verses, things that God shows you to apply in your life, and what happened during the day and how you felt about it.

Keeping A Journal

Keeping a journal is important because you will see how your life is changing. By writing down your prayer needs or other people's needs, you will be able to keep a record of God's answers to your prayers.

When you memorize Scripture, you will be hiding God□s Word in your heart and those verses will keep you from sin. The verses you memorize will comfort you when you are depressed, lonely, fearful, or experience other emotions.

You need to have Scripture handy to resist Satan's attacks. Just claim verses for your life and Satan will flee. He hates to hear God's Word. The most important area is to ask God to show you how to apply what He shows you in His Word. If you do not apply God's Word to your life, you will learn the facts and not develop your relationship with God.

Giving Up Or Pressing Onward

Giving up will not help you. Pressing onward could lead you to eternal life. The decision is up to you. God gave you a free will to do what you wanted with your life. However, if you want to have the best things in life, then you need to choose to follow God. He created you so He knows what is best for your life.

In my life, I wanted to give up several times, but I kept pressing onward hoping to find what would satisfy my desires.

Pressing Onward Leads To Success

Even though I struggled throughout my life, I did have some major successes. It was hard for me to believe that I could be successful at anything because everything seemed to be coming against me. As a result, I was glad that I continued to press onward instead of giving up.

In 1978, I met a piano teacher at Kansas University when my mother and I were there for the National Guild of Piano Auditions. My mother was the chairman of the Lawrence and Topeka chapter at that time. I decided to move to Lawrence and go to Kansas University because I was impressed with the campus, and I wanted to study piano with the teacher I met.

When I enrolled at Kansas University, I decided to major in Human Development and Family Life and work toward an Early Childhood Education Certificate. This certificate would enable me to become a preschool teacher and maybe a director of a center.

However, during my senior year, I became discouraged because I did not receive the encouragement I needed to continue my degree and Early Childhood Education Certificate. After talking to one of my teachers, whom I felt close to because of all the help he had given me in his class, I decided to work for a BGS degree (Bachelor of General Studies) in Human Development and Family Life. Since my degree was a general degree, I could not be a director in a preschool center, but I felt this was the only thing I could do at the time. Finally, in 1981, I graduated from Kansas University, which was my first real success in life.

After that time, I continued to struggle with finances and my spiritual life. In 1982, I moved back to Topeka and bought a house there. I lived there for ten years. In 1992, I was evicted and had to move back home with my parents.

Even though that was a difficult time for me, I adjusted to my circumstances and found the purpose for moving back home.

I became a caregiver for my mother in 1999 until she passed away in May 1999. After that, I was my father's caregiver until he passed away in June 2005.

During my mother's illness, I worked on my second degree, a BA Degree in English with a writing emphasis. I graduated from Washburn in 1999, the same week my mother passed away. That was a difficult time, but I had my second major success in my life, and my mother knew I was going to graduate.

Now, I am living in the house where I lived in since 1956. I am presently working as a substitute teacher, freelance writer, and piano teacher. My desire was to become a published writer, and that has happened in my life.

I also found a church that I like, and my dad's family and I were brought back together again at my mother's funeral. We continued to develop our relationship over the years. God has worked in my life. I accepted Christ as my Savior and Lord on September 27, 1987.

My mother was a Christian and is in heaven, and my father accepted Christ on May 23, 2005, which was a few weeks before he passed away on June 15, 2005.

After his death, I just happened to notice something on their stone. It says: Together Forever. I could not believe it. I had not noticed it before. It really ministered to me when I saw that because I realized they are together forever. I will see them someday.

Since I continued to press onward, I began meeting my goals. You can meet your goals if you continue to press onward and not give up. I hope you have enjoyed by book, and it has ministered to you. Remember--**DON'T GIVE UP--PRESS ONWARD TO KNOW CHRIST.**

> (14) *I press on toward the goal for the*
> *prize of the upward call of God in*
> *Christ Jesus.*
> (Philippians 3:14)

Epilogue

After my father passed away in 2005, I became closer to my cousins, and I helped take care of my uncle, my dad's brother, at times. I enjoyed helping him and getting to know him better. He was also interested in my writing and would always ask me about it when we were together. That blessed me a lot.

In February 2007, my uncle passed away, which was extremely difficult for me because I had just had two years with him and getting to know him after my father passed away. However, I am at peace because my uncle and his wife are in heaven, and my mother and father are also together in heaven as well as my other relatives who have accepted Christ as their Savior and Lord.

Also, in June 2007, I had my first two books published, which was a major success in my life. In July 2007, I had two more books published.

I finally met my goal and would not have met it if I gave up. I kept pressing onward so that I could be successful and reach my goal in life. I am continuing to press onward so that I can keep writing and have more books published.

You can reach your goals in your life if you remember to press onward and not give up.

www.ingramcontent.com/pod-product-compliance
Lightning Source LLC
LaVergne TN
LVHW011246080426
835509LV00005B/642